D1096156

Vienna Choir Boys

Vienna Choir Boys

Edited by Franz Endler
Photographs by Fritz Simak
Translated
by Stephen Temmer

EDITION WIEN

ISBN 3-85058-013-X

Issued also in German under the title: Wiener Sängerknaben

Cover designed by Harry Betke
Photosetting by Quick-Print, Groß-Enzersdorf
Illustrations reproduced by Repro-Brüll, Saalfelden
Printed in Austria by Theissdruck, Wolfsberg

Photographs by Fritz Simak (Cover, pp. 25–32, 49, 53, 54, 56, 73,
74 beneath, 75 beneath, 76–79, 81, 84–88, 105–112) and by Archiv
der Wiener Sängerknaben (pp. 17–24, 50–52, 55, 74 above, 75,
80, 82, 83).

CONTENTS

Translator's Preface

In translating a book about such a tradition-rich organization as the Vienna Choir Boys, one always faces the difficult decision of whether to use the names of places, organizations and the like in its original German, or whether to make a best effort at translating everything into English. In this book we have largely maintained the original German names, "umlauts" (those two little marks above an a, o, or u) and all, with very few exceptions, notably "Lake Wörthersee" which literally means "Lake Wörther Lake."

We do have to explain an important thing to you. The English translation for the „Wiener Sängerknaben," the proper German name for our Institute, varies throughout the world. In every English speaking country, except for the United States of America, they are called "Vienna Boys' Choir." In the U.S.A., and nowhere else, they are called the "Vienna Choir Boys." There is really no logical explanation except for the fact that Sol Hurok, the original management organization who toured the choir throughout the U.S.A. shortly after it was reorganized after World War II, had the name "Vienna Choir Boys" entered as a registered trade mark in the United States. And so it is that the name has remained. In view of the fact that your translator lives in New York City, he has taken the prerogative of using the American name.

Incidentally, it saves him the trouble of that nasty apostrophe after "Boys'". The only other words we'd like to clarify are as follows:

Hofmusikkapelle (Imperial Music Chapel) = Court Music Choir as well as the Organization. This is the organization which has traditionally cared for the musical life of the (here's that other German word we always use . . .)

Hofburgkapelle = Imperial Court Chapel.

The Hofmusikkapelle consists of the Vienna Philharmonic Orchestra, the Vienna State Opera Chorus, and, of course, the Vienna Choir Boys.

Now that you know all that, we wish you a great deal of enjoyment in your reading of our Vienna Choir Boys book.

Prof. Stephen F. Temmer
former Vienna Choir Boy

January 1987

Two Addresses in Vienna

I

Hofmusikkapelle, I, Hofburg, Schweizerhof.

This address means a great deal in a country which is based on tradition, which lives off tradition and thinks a lot of tradition. It is true that there are still a few singers and actors around who have the right to call themselves „Hofschauspieler" (court actors) or „Mitglieder des Hofoperntheaters" (members of the court opera theater) because they entered their profession at a time when their top boss was the emperor. While it is true that one still awards the title of „Hofrat" in the Republic of Austria, a title which appears to indicate that one is at court, in the immediate vicinity of the emperor, and that one's counsel and advice is valued there, the rest of the former titles and other outward signs, which might remind one of a world empire, have fallen by the wayside. After both of this century's wars, most institutions and later all of the citizens have had their titles revoked. The court opera became the state opera, the court riding school's Lipizzans were converted into the white steeds of the Spanish Riding School, and the „Baron" became a simple „Herr Doktor."

The Hofmusikkapelle holds true to its tradition and continues under its old name, at its old location, and in a form which has remained virtually unchanged for centuries. No one could, no one wished to assail its traditions, something which is an inimitable part of its substance. So it was that even the "republican" officials were resigned, and listed it in the telephone book under its true title:

Hofmusikkapelle, I, Hofburg, Schweizerhof.

If one clings to documentation, if one demands accurate data, black on white, in order to celebrate jubilees, then one must calculate the Hofmusikkapelle's age from 20 July 1498. This date is connected with a decree by Emperor Maximilian I, which states in no uncertain terms, how the „Hofmusikkapelle" in Vienna is to be organized and how it is to function. In actuality this founding decree is a document in the history of an institution which had already existed previously: life at court without music was unthinkable even prior to the 20th of July 1498, and there have always been singers and musicians available for both sacred and secular feasts. One could delve further into history and unearth Viennese documents about musicians and label them the legitimate predecessors of today's Hofmusikkapelle. However, history has decided to look upon the date of the above mentioned founding decree from 1498 as the Hofmusikkapelle's birth date.

Effective with that year, the songs in honor of God and often also to the glory of Vienna's rulers, have never been silenced. If one wants to assume that the heart of Vienna, the music city, resides either at the opera house, at which legends battle as if for sleeping beauty's castle, or if one is inclined to assume that the center of tradition resides in that honored institution the Gesellschaft der Musikfreunde (the Society of the Friends of Music) with its members Schubert, Beethoven, Brahms, and Bruckner, there nevertheless remains the incontrovertible fact that the nucleus of all musical tradition, in truth, centers on the Hofmusikkapelle.

Continuity is a magic word at the Hofmusikkapelle. The emperor's sires wrote music for its boys' choir and took care of their education. Those monarchs less interested in music, in the end also Franz Josef I., "the last gentleman on a throne of Europe," as Roosevelt called him, nevertheless held to tradition and made certain that the Hofmusikkapelle remained that place where they spoke to their God and the choir boys accompanied with song. The emperor's household attended Sunday mass in the strict, cool Court Chapel. Here, too, the choir boys sang the responses when a member of the imperial household had died. The emperor who was to live through desperate times, at the last even World War I, was not very musically inclined. Nevertheless the Hofmusikkapelle existed even under his patronage. Also unchanged under Franz Josef I. was the rule that he who served his emperor had his uniform and his duties, but also the continuing protection of his master. As long as the financial means sufficed and the singer's or musician's behavior did not leave anything to be desired, a member of the Hofmusikkapelle had an assured standard of living, even when he could no longer sing or play. In spite of the attempt to intensify the connection between the Hofmusikkapelle and the court opera theater, and to employ the adult singers and musicians at both institutions, both the soprano and alto voices were sung by specially trained boys, just as Emperor Maximilan I. had decreed back in 1498. Boys with their clean, clear, innocent voices appeared more suitable to the mass than did bosomed female voices (perhaps this inspired Mozart to write his masses, or remained in the foreground when Bruckner wrote his works), and so the Hofburgkapelle (Imperial Court Chapel) remained the one place where women had to keep quiet.

This church law was originally intended to apply only to the mass celebrants, but was also forced upon the musicians and has been observed for these past hundreds of years. Boys and castrates sang in place of women and indeed a great deal of old music is written for their voices. The result was a rather unusual, specific choral sound. One only has to hear a mass sung by a women's chorus and then in the Hofburgkapelle to understand the difference.

One may perhaps believe that it is only the Vienna Choir Boys in its present form which form the principal attraction to the Sunday masses in the Hofburgkapelle, I, Schweizerhof. One is in error. It has always been a significant, never abrogated component of a musical mass, that boys sang. Vienna the music city has always had church choirs; even those of astonishing size. Music was practiced far into the suburbs Sunday after Sunday with great devotion and excellence. In the emperor's chapel, however, in the true center of the city, it was especially selected boys who sang. It is a fact that in Austria, yes even in Vienna, there have been boys' choirs again and again.

Above all it was the youngsters who attended parochial schools who most often were assembled into choirs of acknowledged proficiency. It is the continuity, however, the permanent preservation of music and the musical tradition, and with it the assurance of continuity in the art of singing, that was assigned to the Hofmusikkapelle. Throughout the centuries, in constant service at one and the same spot; there is no better sign for musical aristocracy which has stood and still stands the test of time.

The downfall of the Habsburg empire could have meant the death knell for the Hofmusikkapelle. In fact in 1918 the choir boys were sent home and the required singers for the masses were obtained from among the ladies of the state opera chorus. But just as men were found right after the collapse of the monarchy who believed in the continuity of the opera, and the friends of music, who turned unrealized plans into reality and who founded the Salzburg Festivals, so a man stepped forward who saved the tradition of the Hofmusikkapelle by founding a new institution to preserve the old.

Josef Schnitt from Mailberg, Austria, an ecclesiastic appointed the rector of the Hofmusikkapelle in 1921, made it his aim in life to preserve the mass at the Hofmusikkapelle according to the rules set down in 1498. He contributed everything he owned, and to the end of his days his entire energy to that cause. Vienna must thank him for the fact that the Hofmusikkapelle still exists today in its original form. One must thank his boundless energy and also the very special circumstances under which this energy had to prove itself, that besides the centuries old institution, there now exists a second one, which belongs to Vienna: The Vienna Choir Boys. This more or less lay institution, nevertheless inimitably tied to ecclesiastic service, likely never would have been created, had it not been for Rector Schnitt's desire to have the Boys' Choir for his Hofburgkapelle, and had the world economic crisis not forced him to support these choir boys by letting them sing outside the Hofburg, as the "Vienna Choir Boys."

Albrecht Dürer's woodcut of Emperor Maximilian I., who founded the
Vienna Choir Boys by imperial decree in 1498.

II

There are fixed points of interest on the itinerary of every tourist who wants to discover Vienna. He who does not cover them has not seen the city according to a majority opinion. Just as in every spot on earth, these are attractions which one may visit according to a certain scheme and cleverly conceived tourist time schedule, but which do not appear to the locals – e.g. the Viennese – as so particularly significant. The fact that someone who visits Vienna would also like to climb the tower of St. Stephen's cathedral, is something no Viennese has ever considered.

Those attractions in Vienna are easily and quickly enumerated: an opera visit is unavoidable, a visit to the Kunsthistorische Museum (Museum of Fine Arts), a bus trip through the Vienna woods with but a minute's pause at Mayerling, the locale of the presumed suicide pact between crown prince Rudolf and his beloved, and a longer rest stop on Vienna's mountain, the Kahlenberg. Then there's a visit to the Schönbrunn Palace, and for the evening a "Heurigen" visit to taste the new wine. On Sunday there is an obligatory attendance at the Hofburgkapelle and right afterwards a visit to the Spanish Riding School. The last places to visit mentioned are those for which, according to the Viennese, "there aren't any tickets available anyway." All these are visits to places which are typically Viennese, but are firmly in the tourists' hands, which is why most of the Viennese really no longer try to gain access to them. Both of the latter institutions are considered very exclusive due to the fact that room is severely limited. Tickets for the Lipizzan horses and for the masses at the Hofburgkapelle are scarcer than tickets for an evening at the state opera. The Lipizzans perform twice each week, while the mass performance at the Hofburgkapelle takes place only on Sunday mornings, although that the whole year round with the exception of the two summer months, during which the opera is closed as well and the children are on vacation.

Sunday after Sunday there is singing at the Hofburgkapelle, while on about sixty afternoons throughout the year there are small receptions for convention participants, tourist groups, or other groups which had made timely bookings to come to the Augarten Palace, the home of the Vienna Choir Boys. Oratorios for which boys' voices are required are performed frequently at the Musikverein, Vienna's large concert hall, and the smaller Konzerthaus. At the State Opera, too, there are many works requiring one or more singing boys. Hofmusikkapelle, Augarten Palace, Musikverein, Konzerthaus, State Opera: the singing of the Vienna Choir Boys may be heard everywhere, and yet there are many average Viennese who steadfastly believe that the Vienna Choir Boys are a touring chorus, which is under way somewhere in the world singing Strauß waltzes. It is these same average Viennese who don't even notice the St. Stephen's cathedral, and who drive around the Ringstraße without realizing that they are being offered a panorama of world historic significance. Why then should they even notice the Vienna Choir Boys in the Hofburgkapelle or elsewhere?

The Vienna Choir Boys, that isn't ten or twenty soloists whose names are known to every taxi driver and whose private lives are the topic of conversation for the entire city. It also isn't near one hundred esteemed professors, who are much in demand by every music buff of the city, as is the case with the members of the Vienna Philharmonic. They are many, many boys – there are at least one hundred – who just at this moment represent the active Vienna Choir Boys, and beyond that numerous boys who are studying to become choir boys; and finally they are countless former choir boys who never have lost contact with their childhood, and who, even in their adult years refer to themselves as former choir boys. Aside from that one must add many adults under the banner of the Vienna Choir Boys who have never sung at all: conductors, teachers, prefects, nurses who accompany the choir on its trips, the personnel which runs the institution, and finally the Director of the choir who runs everything. Only when one has considered that they all contribute to the concept of the Vienna Choir Boys, one has defined the perimeter. Twenty-four boys standing about a piano and conducted by a choir master, twenty-four boys in sailor suits, that is a touring choir. A trade mark. All the boys and all the adults together are really the Vienna Choir Boys.

It is only possible in this way to explain why the concept exists, while great value is placed at the Vienna Choir Boys on anonymity. Internally one is aware of every soloist's name and discusses his great deeds, while on the outside the name Vienna Choir Boys is used even when only three of them sing in "The Magic Flute." This is the explanation of why one may know a single choir boy without knowing anything about the institution, while one knows the concept of Vienna Choir Boys, without being able to report about the fate of any individual boy in it.

Is it generally known that it is becoming ever more difficult to find Vienna Choir Boys? Is one able to guess how someone becomes a Vienna Choir Boy? Does one not expect completely false things when one decides to become a choir boy? Can one even make such a decision?

Hardly ever has any boy made a decision himself to become a Vienna Choir Boy. And that's perfectly natural when one considers that children of six or seven hardly have any career wishes. It is the parents, relatives, and teachers who sense a special musical talent or a pretty voice, or who simply have the desire to make a boy into a choir boy. This institutions which previously recruited almost exclusively from Vienna, now takes children from all over Austria. Times are ever changing: those which give the appearance that there are hardly enough talented boys are followed by those which appear to be "better." However, it cannot be denied that in families, yes even in Viennese families, there is less singing than ever before. Future Vienna Choir Boys will not be formed as easily in front of a television screen.

A further problem is represented by the phenomenon of acceleration. The ever more rapid maturing of the boys, who are reminded daily of the fact that they will shortly turn into men, brings with it a body reaction of earlier maturity. This phenomenon is not solely to be observed in choir boys, but rather is to be found in all present day children, who have found it fashionable to accelerate the maturing process, in fact all natural processes. This, in turn, results in these few musically talented boys being available to the choir for ever shorter periods of time. The Vienna Choir Boys always have four completely trained choirs available at the same time in order to be able to meet their obligations both for tours and for the many assignments in and around Vienna. They must take into account an ever more rapid change of generations and therefore must look for new talent even more diligently.

This activity is under no circumstance a matter of pure pleasure, but rather singing at the highest professional level, which may not ever slip into the area of child's play. The word professional is certainly properly applied. In selecting the boys in Vienna and the rest of Austria, it is important to bear in mind that the Vienna Choir Boys are not merely any kind of boys' choir, but is judged in all the world according to an entirely different standard, and that they have more to do than merely to sing. They must not only be better and more multi facetted than other choirs, but above that they must fulfill for their entire tour the expectations of their observers. There have indeed been cases when the Institute had to decline a very talented choir boy simply because he was unable to shed his dialect, which led to the predictable situation that he would only be able to integrate himself with great difficulty into the society life of the choir, and this, in turn, would have possibly made him an aberration in the spotlight of public life. It is their travels which is the more important thing to the Vienna Choir Boys. These are also a tradition, if one reads the history of the Hofmusikkapelle. Emperors ordered their musicians to attend their state affairs or sent them to friendly courts elsewhere.

Travels in today's style represent more: they are the only way of securing the existence of the institution of the Vienna Choir Boys. The boys bring back from their travels not only recollections, but also above all the money which is so necessary for the maintenance of the institute and with it, the existence of the Hofmusikkapelle. The performance of the Vienna Choir Boys at the

*U*ntil the end of the monarchy, the Vienna Choir Boys, in appropriate uniforms, were a part of the imperial court.

*M*onsignore Josef Schnitt founded the Vienna Choir Boys (again) in 1924 and remained the Choir's director until his death in 1955.

*T*he boys in Mozart's "Bastien und Bastienne".
Beneath: Their long-time artistic director Ferdinand Grossmann during instruction.

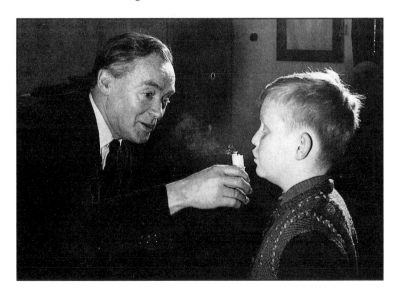

*T*he Choir Boys in their Palace and during an oratorio in the Vienna Konzerthaus.

*T*heir most important duty: a mass in the Imperial Chapel under the baton of the former musical director, Dr. Hans Gillesberger.

Together with the Chorus Viennensis, made up of former members of the Choir, in the Imperial Chapel.

*P*ictures taken during world tours: in front of the Towerbridge in London and of the Eiffel Tower in Paris.

*O*nce every year the Vienna Choir Boys are in the States to give several concerts. Japan on the other hand has got to wait for them sometimes up to two years.

*T*he "Josefstöckl" in the vast grounds around the Augarten Palace. Here the Vienna Choir Boys receive their basic musical education in a special grammar school.

*E*xercises which teach a professional singer the important breathing techniques.

*S*port activities are the much needed compensation in the life of every Choir Boy.

Choir Boys are just like other children when it comes to school work: they have to think.

*B*oth schooling and physical education take place in the most modern surroundings.

A positive experience: eating together with many other boys furthers the appetite.

*T*he Vienna Choir Boys have all of the modern conveniences available to them.

*C*hoir Boys out of uniform are just like all other boys, thank God.

Sunday masses, at oratorios, and at performances of the state opera could not take place, if these cultural institutions were compelled to pay the real costs of supplying the Vienna Choir Boys' services. The maintenance of the boarding facilities, the basic requirement for maintaining a choir of world class, can only be assured through the organization of four choirs of which at least two are constantly on tour, bringing in the needed funds. Only choir boys can maintain choir boys. The birth of the Hofmusikkapelle is assumed to be at the time of the decree of Emperor Maximilian I., and one has become accustomed to look upon the founding of their successors, the Vienna Choir Boys as the time when Rector Schnitt began to hold auditions for a boys' choir for the Hofmusikkapelle. Then, when Rector Schnitt permitted his boys to rehearse a children's opera, when he accepted offers from overseas, in other words when he found during the tough twenties, the only way to assure a well organized musical education and boarding school, it was then that the institution of Vienna Choir Boys in its present form was founded.

It is a clear habit of all former Vienna choir boys that they remember best of all their personal time as Vienna choir boys, and that they continuously brag about the fact and insist that their particular time at the choir was indeed the big time of Vienna Choir Boys. There are gentlemen who remember the time before the great depression and who believe that only in the first and second generation there were really great soloists and never to be repeated performances. There is no problem finding gentlemen in Vienna who sang as Vienna choir boys during World War II – Rector Schnitt was relieved of his directorate of the Institute – however the responsible ones of that era had great difficulty to keep choir and politics apart and to maintain a continuity at the Hofmusikkapelle. They too rave about their era at the choir. There are former choir boys who lived through the second post war era of this century as children, again with Rector Schnitt and again under conditions which remind one of the founders' period. They too speak of great soloists in their midst, of specially qualified choir masters, and of incredible tour adventures.

To produce an all encompassing book about the past more than sixty years of the Vienna Choir Boys, a book that would satisfy everyone, it would be necessary that all of the generations which grew up during those sixty years participate in its writing.

Of course it is a fact that former choir boys only recognize as adults the meaning of the institution to which they belonged. This institution primarily and forever exists in the close ties with the great tradition of that other institution, the Hofmusikkapelle. The heads of the Vienna Choir Boys, first Rector Schnitt, then Hofrat Tautschnig and now his successor Walter Tautschnig, have always looked upon this close tie as a conditio sine qua non. After all, Rector Schnitt newly founded the boys' choir, and with it the institution in an effort to again perform the mass at the Hofburg in its traditional form. He spent his entire life in discussions or the exchange of letters of an official character, in an effort to make perfectly clear to government officials the meaning of the Hofmusikkapelle and the participation of boys' voices at mass. He always had to fight against the same opponent, who sat in the high offices already during the emperor's reign, and who made the choir boys' existence more difficult. One had a great deal of understanding for the Hofmusikkapelle and the Vienna Choir Boys during the time of the First Republic; understanding, but little money. And an institution of the dimensions of the Hofmusikkapelle can not be maintained simply with the understanding tolerance of government officials. One needs above all the understanding and hopefully unbureaucratic financial support.

Hofrat Dr. Tautschnig, the successor to Rector Schnitt, a former Vienna Choir Boy of the first generation, and therefore well familiar with all of the problems, finally brought some order out of the financial chaos. There are now contracts, regulations about rehearsals, binding agreements, and above all this, a very important official declaration: The boys' choir now singing at the Hofburg, is now officially looked upon as the sole heir to the former k.k. (royal and imperial) Court Boys' Choir. Only the Vienna Choir Boys may supply the choir for the Hofburg and only they have the right to tell all the world that they alone are the choir which Maximilan I. specifically mentioned in his decree of 1498. Whatever the Vienna Choir Boys are aside from all that: singing ambassadors of their country, travellers in matters music, singing angels, or whatever one wants to call them, they are first and foremost the heirs to a tradition. They are both the guaranty for the fact that the Hofmusikkapelle as an institution is not a secular and an ecclesiastic treasure house, but rather remains a living space within the confines of the Vienna Royal City Castle. Modern composers still write masses for the Vienna Choir Boys, and they alone make sure that they are performed. St. Stephan's Cathedral organist, Peter Planyavsky, has dedicated his "Missa Viennensis" to them, while new sacred works by Stravinsky, Krenek, Heiller, and J. N. David have been heard at the Hofburg. However, one may not make the false assumption that the Hofburgkapelle is a revolutionary place, where the development of music is practiced every Sunday. The Second Vatican Council, which also steered music along new paths without making a clear statement about its future, has had a revolutionary effect here. If one were to observe its dictates strictly, then one would no longer be allowed to perform a mass written by any of the old masters during services; only the people's music and music for the new liturgy would be allowed. But as is usually the case, one tries to obtain exceptions from strict rules, and so it was that a papal decree specifically recognizes the Hofmusikkapelle as an institution where music of the old style is to be preserved. Not only on the church's high holidays, and not intermingled with newly introduced practices, but rather consciously and proudly one continues to celebrate every Sunday with music in the old style. It is indeed a high mass which the numerous visitors are privileged to experience.

Concessions were made to accommodate the wishes of the visitors rather than the new performance practice and the new liturgy. Television monitors have been installed in the oratorios of the chapel according to a layout which permits those who for many years have sat patiently squeezed into their seats, able only to hear the ringing of the bells from below and the music from above, now clearly to see both the mass celebrants and the members of the Hofmusikkapelle. The administration of the Hofburgkapelle has no illusions. One has admitted freely that many visitors do not come because of their religious zeal and some not even for their love for the music of Mozart or Schubert, but rather because they want to attend "The Mass of the Vienna Choir Boys."

Concessions as a sign of commercial thinking? He who has harsh words to utter for this is not only an odd dreamer, but he rather ignores those performances which the Vienna Choir Boys offer in the Hofburgkapelle. Evening concerts of sacred music, many times of an avant-garde, progressive nature. Not so much as an attraction, and certainly not understood in that way, but rather as the fulfillment of a duty which everyone assumes who enters into the great traditions of the Hofburgkapelle.

It is not the boys who do that, but rather the administration of the Institution Vienna Choir Boys who think of this, since they are responsible for the preservation of the tradition, the continuous development of the music and the assurance of financial viability of the Hofmusikkapelle. The tradition, that the official or secret first conductor of the city not only directs the opera, but also the Hofmusikkapelle, has remained a fact over time. Even after World War II is was clearly understood that Joseph Krips, who without rank and title, but nevertheless with his full personal zeal, conducted most of the important concerts and a large portion of all the opera performances in Vienna, still found time for the Vienna Choir Boys. The practice of using opera personnel for the bass and tenor voices as well as for the musicians, is still intact today. Since it is likely that Vienna choir boys enter the music field after their service with the Vienna Choir Boys has ended, it is not surprising that one finds former choir boys in the choir – among the basses and tenors – and in the orchestra of the Hofmusikkapelle. For other former Vienna choir boys the

Choralschola was created, which sings the proprium down below next to the high altar. And still more other boys' choir members serve behind the scenes: they are active in the organization, or return every Sunday as ushers or at the box office at the place where they had sung Palestrina or Bruckner many years before.

There also are Vienna choir boys among the congregation. When the mass is over and the visitors have left the chapel and pour out into the Schweizerhof of the City Court, small groups gather for a few minutes from among those for whom attendance at mass has become a beloved habit, to hold a kind of "club meeting" and to exchange memories and experiences. It is among this group that one finds the severest critics. Experienced, knowledgeable, connected to the institution in enduring gratefulness – but quite wide awake. Those masses which find approval by former Vienna choir boys are of very special note.

This serendipitous meeting in the Schweizerhof is not the only kind of get together; there is also the Association of the Vienna Choir Boys. Firstly because every institution must have a legal framework; secondly because even a private, independent institution must have a corporate form to which it is responsible; and thirdly because people, beginning at a certain age, search for and maintain associations, often recognizing that boyhood friendships represent closer friendships than those formed in later life. The Association of the Vienna Choir Boys has by-laws, among which the most important prerequisite for membership is that one must have been a Vienna choir boy. All initial plans to arrange this Association in some other way, perhaps to give it the patronage or attention of personalities in high places or important personages, were quickly set aside. Anyone who is to have a voice in shaping, even marginally, what the Vienna Choir Boys are to do, must have been a Vienna choir boy, must have sung at the Hofburg, must have known the choir's travels, must know whereof he speaks in such a meeting.

In spite of this important membership prerequisite, there is still quite a variety to be found among its members. Relatively few Vienna choir boys later become musicians. Both in the Association as well as the unofficial meetings after the Sunday mass at the Hofburg, one may find representatives of every walk of life, of every level of society. Former Vienna choir boys are employed in banking, and they concern themselves with the financial health of the institution. Some became architects: and one of these built a vacation home for the Vienna Choir Boys and all of the buildings which surround the Augarten Palace. Some have studied medicine and concern themselves with the choir boys' health.

But there are always other choir boys, who later again live at the Institute as prefects, and who, after their studies at the Music Academy, the Conservatory of Music, become choir masters at the Vienna Choir Boys, and naturally they are very successful, since they know from personal experience how to handle the boys. The choir's management is firmly in the hands of former choir members: first there was Hofrat Tautschnig, a former choir boy, prefect, and confidant of Rector Schnitt, who took over the choir after Schnitt's death. He was followed by his son Walter Tautschnig jr., and he is now the director of the Institute. Besides his many other qualifications, he too was a Vienna choir boy, and therefore had a lifelong connection with the Hofburgkapelle, Augarten Palace and travels around the globe. Who is better able to concern himself with the Vienna Choir Boys than a former choir boy?

Naturally this book, as well, has been written and photographed (and translated) by former Vienna choir boys: Fritz Simak was a Vienna choir boy and studied trumpet before deciding to go into photography. The author of these lines served in the choir starting in 1948, and is therefore connected with the Institute in his own, and ofttimes selfcritical, way. As a music critic he has only rarely had the duty to write anything other than hymns of praise for his successors. My time as a Vienna Choir Boy – for just a short moment I'd like to sound a personal note – coincided with the first few years of the post World

War II era. Rector Schnitt had again assumed his duties as director of the Institute, the opulent times at the Wilhelminenberg Castle and the rather comfortable ones at the Mariatheresien Palace were over. The choir boys again lived at the place where they had lived at the time of their founding: the Hofburg. A very large and more than adequate new home, the Augarten Palace, had just been found and was being renovated with moneys from current income. All around the chapel were grouped rehearsal rooms, class rooms and a dining room. One flight up, immediately below the roof, with a view of the imperial gardens, were the sleeping accommodations. Such things as play rooms, gymnasiums or similar luxuries were not even dreamed of. The entire City Castle was the territory for forbidden and enticing excursions from the choir boys' day to day atmosphere. The castle is a city in itself, with many narrow corridors under the roof, where once the servants were quartered, and where now lived government employees. There were opulent stairways or very narrow, unexpected corridors leading outdoors. One could either get lost or explore the Hofburg like a labyrinth. One usually found one's way back home after some of these exciting explorations, but one often aroused the indignation of fellow tenants, who had to tolerate a horde of boys storming past their door. In the imperial gardens there was an openair theater arranged by the Soviet occupation forces, whose films were impossible to understand and were rather boring as well, but which could be observed – even though forbidden – from the dormitory rooms.

Towards the end of Sunday mass, there wafted through the Hofburgkapelle not only the lingering odor of incense, but also that of roast pork and cabbage. We ate in the rooms where today the musicians tune up and perhaps a cellist rehearses a last minute phrase. We "old-timers" for years have sorely missed the precursory odors of a hearty lunch towards the end of the high mass. Generations who have come after us know nothing of this feeling of longing.

That very natural combination of those rooms in which one lives, works, and rehearses with those in which one appears before the public and must learn to behave oneself, are a component of every choir boy's "home" and is a basic component of the Institute's behavior education. A choir boy should feel comfortable while studying and have every opportunity for activity during his free time. However, he should also learn how to behave himself in surroundings which deviate a great deal from the daily life. He must learn that. Once the boys are under way in their uniform, whether in Vienna or in a foreign land, they are immediately admired and observed in every conceivable situation. This might well go to their heads, make them unsure of themselves, or trigger affected behavior, were they not schooled carefully, day by day, in the way to appear in public. He who is at home in the ornate rooms of the Vienna Hofburg, or has ascended or descended the grand staircase at the Augarten Palace, will learn quickly to behave naturally and unaffectedly. Nevertheless he will not forget how to play soccer, how to wrestle during his free time, can still climb trees and is not in danger of becoming a softy or a wimp. He simply feels just as at home in large hotel lobbies or at official receptions overseas, as he does at the playground. He has the natural behavior of a boy and above that still a bit of the attributes of an old fashioned cavalier.

It is their surroundings which cause the Vienna Choir Boys to get along well among themselves. As a result they adjust well to any situation with the general public and therefore also with one another. The danger that their origins might create difficulties, that within the choir there might arise social tension, has simply never materialized. When they appear in public they all wear the same sailor uniform, which should not be taken as a reminder of imperial times when the monarchy was a sea power, but rather as a reminder of earlier days when Austrian boys from good homes wore sailor suits. When they are at home there simply is no possibility of sticking out of the crowd: boys' pants remain boys' pants and a sweater is always a sweater.

Extravagances are out of the question and fashion is not of interest to boys between ten and fourteen. Living in the boarding school environment in no way suppresses personality, but rather makes them better able to get along and to be each other's pals. The daily rehearsals underline the fact that music is the most important thing. Whether a choir boy is an only child and spoiled, or whether his parents are wealthy, that is of no interest to the other boys. How he sings, that's what's interesting. How he plays soccer may also be important.

Street car conductors have sent their boys to the choir just as has the aristocracy. In times of need it was not unimportant for parents to have one less mouth to feed, and to know that their child was in good hands. In relatively or absolutely good times, this attraction drops away, and the Institute, on the contrary, must offer some luxuries to motivate parents to send their child to the choir. What's important remains is that one belongs to the Vienna Choir Boys to make music and to travel. But above all to make music – both in good and bad times.

If one must make differentiations, then it is between those boys from Vienna who may go home to their parents over the weekend, and those boys from other states, who must remain at the Institute on Saturdays and Sundays as well. It has never been investigated whether the Viennese boys have the advantage or whether it is those boys who profit by always being together. Serious homesickness is relatively rare among the boys. One surely must be from the world of film and must be looking for a subject for a Vienna Choir Boys' film, to be able to construct conflicts and tragedy from their lifestyle. How else can one explain that when the boys' voices change, when they are unable to sing anymore, they ofttimes don't want to go home, but rather stay as "mutants" at the Augarten Palace? Only through habit? Like so many other things, this too is only a matter of conjecture, and yet one may determine: in the Vienna Choir Boys one just isn't homesick. One doesn't even think about being anything else but a Vienna choir boy. One feels great for a long list of reasons, and if asked quickly, couldn't mention any of them. That's just the way it is.

Music theory is only a minor subject during the preparatory training. The main topic is the child's voice, which is to get the right "set" through practice. One is concerned with proper breathing while singing. Today everyone must learn to read music. In prior days most of the children already knew that when they came into the choir boy courses. The children are taught to sight read, using time honored methods; i.e. to sing from notes just as one reads letters, without having to have it played a dozen times. One naturally studies several choral works. The children don't even notice how they are being observed and trained. It only becomes a sensation for them when the preparatory time has ended, when they have spent a summer in the Vienna Choir Boys' vacation village and have been assigned to a choir. In earlier times Rector Schnitt took a boy from the reserve choir by the hand, brought him into a rehearsal room, and simply sat him down next to the others, the longest tenured choir boys. Usually the choir master bid adieu to another choir member at the same time, and the general excitement about the changes lasted no more than a half hour. Today there is a kind of ritual: the director presents to the new choir boy his first uniform, which he soon will outgrow. Since one has learned from earlier conversations with the director, just how important the uniform is, one receives it with pride and with the same degree of excitement as all of those who have been accepted by the Vienna Choir Boys in the past fifty years.

From that moment on, the rhythm, the daily schedule changes. However, not the training, not the constant and hopefully unobtrusive education in every area, but above all in the areas of music and singing. Even active choir boys go through their daily vocalizing; they are observed and improved upon. Under ideal conditions and with steady application of good technique, a Vienna Choir Boy could sing to a ripe old age, to be able to smoothly master the transition from one register to another. In the personnel files one can find the name Kurt Equiluz, whose technique one ofttimes praised in oratorios. He was a Vienna choir boy and continued to sing without a change of voice. Not in the sense which journalists may mean when they predict the end of a „Wunderkind" career. They simply have to say "change of voice" and the man in the street, as well as musicians who are not educated in this field, immediately think of hoarseness, a cracking into falsetto and immediately of a bass. That all is really not necessary. A choir boy who has always sung well may be carefully led, while in a choir, from the soprano to the alto voice, and might then even continue as a tenor, baritone or bass. His voice really never has to "crack." He simply changes his voice range.

It is one of the success recipes of the Vienna Choir Boys Institution not to burden the boys with theory. One simply applies the experiences of many years and allows nature to participate in the formulation of the voice. The few rules one has to learn and understand are in no way complicated. One must breathe properly, one must support the tone correctly; one will be led by the choir master until the voice "sits" properly. When singing teachers all over the world try to sell their particular theories or methods as the true secret to success, and try to convince everyone that only they know, then this is usually either superstition or a business tactic. The Vienna Choir Boys have nothing whatsoever to do with any of that.

After his retirement Ferdinand Grossmann, for many years the artistic director of the Institute, recognized as a foremost choir master even outside Austria, and in demand as a musical pedagogue, opened a kind of "elementary art school." He wanted to find boys for the Vienna Choir Boys directly from Kindergarten, and furthermore wanted to prove that one could awaken in every child a talent for singing or at least a sense of the artistic. Ferdinand Grossmann, who had at least a theoretical success with this endeavor, has died. However his experiment has been reactivated, and the Vienna Choir Boys now obtain talent for their ranks from this source.

Grossmann's conclusions, which he drew from today's apparent acceleration of the body's maturing process, are pure illusion. Even if it should come to a time when boys have to quit singing in their thirteenth year, one can hardly advance the time when a boy's choir career might start. Prior to a certain age, it is not possible to integrate a child into the daily routine consisting of school, rehearsal, concert, travel, and again rehearsal. It would simply be counter to nature. The Vienna Choir Boys have tried to consider these facts. They begin their gratis courses earlier and so offer a kind of musical background even to those children who later don't necessarily want to become choir boys. They try to have orderly choirs, but above all members who are not prematurely exhausted „Wunderkinder," but rather with all the professionalism, remain children.

They must remain children, and certainly not to preserve an institution which has been created within the past fifty years, but rather to guarantee the continuity of music. Just as great orchestras, purely because they exist, compel contemporary composers to write for them and to create works of giant proportions, so it is that traditional boys' choirs have the responsibility to motivate composers to write for them.

Musicologists may notice an ambivalence at this point, which we want to clarify. A boys' choir of the Vienna Choir Boys' standing is certainly best able to fulfill the difficult technical requirements which all of the composers who are devoted to progress demand of the artists. One cannot expect this from lay choirs. On the other hand, it is the Vienna Choir Boys' tradition, and the fact that a boys choir's possibilities are not boundless, which forces even progressive composers to move within reasonable boundaries, thereby making a somewhat simpler statement, and one which is more concentrated than could be written for a choir of adults. One has but to hear the Vienna Choir Boys to understand that excellent, new music has been written thanks to their initiative.

Above all the Vienna Choir Boys are the true guarantor for the continuity of the Hofmusikkapelle, and with it the continuity of sacred music in Vienna.

As important as the work of the church music section of the Conservatory may be, or the conservation of sacred music practiced by individuals in Vienna, so it is a fact that every progressive movement requires popular exponents, successful flag bearers. The fact that the Vienna Choir Boys continues to sing the mass at the Hofburg may be termed a tourist stop organized by travel bureaus, if one pays heed to malicious observers. In truth it is an ongoing advertisement for the right of church music to exist.

Who then guarantees the continuity of the Vienna Choir Boys, in light of the enumerated difficulties? Only the Vienna Choir Boys themselves; by traveling around the globe, singing there and in Vienna; by attracting ever more generations of choir boys and by offering them ever better facilities through the realization of successes and the prerequisites for success out of their own strength and without the supervision of some other entity. Their calling card notes two addresses: Hofmusikkapelle, I, Hofburg, Schweizerhof, and one which guarantees their future: Vienna Choir Boys, II, Augarten Palace.

At Home and on Tour

I

In order to be able to explain how and why the Vienna Choir Boys occupies a very special position among all of the choirs of the world, which are known to the world of music or to Vienna, one would have to take a closer look what other boys' choirs exist and how they are organized.

There are a number of boys' choirs in Austria which are formed within a religious order and its abbey. The boys come to a monastery in order to attend school. If it appears that they have a musical talent, they are put in the choir and they become choir boys of "St. Somewhere." Famous and excellent musicians have come from these choirs, from the parochial schools and subsequently have earned much honor for their teachers. On the other hand there are boys in Austria and the rest of the world, who come together once or twice a week to practice choir music. Their choir masters endeavor to obtain engagements for their boys, and some of them go on brief tours and are called upon to perform at local festive occasions. They may perform folk music or something of questionable taste and don't have it easy: first of all, the boys must attend school and can engage in their music only in their spare time. It is easy to understand why the performance level is not quite as exemplary as the thrill of the parents. Boys' choirs of great tradition, on the other hand, those who have great artistic fame to defend, are quite rare.

And finally there are choirs everywhere at churches and schools, which only remain in existence as long as a teacher or organist or minister or school director enjoy choral singing. They are formed casually and dissolve just as casually again. Even if they should "appear in public" for some festive occasion now and then, it is hardly necessary to take note of them, just as one hardly notices some folk music group from across the seas, or some school chorus which may serve a brief stint in "Carmen" because it happens to be located near an opera house in Berlin or Hamburg. None of these choruses may be compared to the Vienna Choir Boys, which continues a 500-year-old tradition and fill it with life. Neither from the standpoint of organization nor from the artistic level. How then does the life of a Vienna choir boy look? The daily routine is comparable to that of a well organized convent. Vienna choir boys, like other children, get up at 6:30 and have time for breakfast before school begins. Since they all get up at the same time, there are fewer problems than would be the case for a single child. A room full of laughter and fun in the morning is more stimulating than a cozy bed at home.

It is a primary rule that children must get enough sleep – both on tour and in Vienna. If a choir or several soloists have been working the night before, then they get an extra portion of sleep. The scheduled classes are not disturbed by this arrangement, but for the school master it means extra work. Nevertheless, he must heed the rule which states that every choir boy must have sufficient sleep.

The morning school session is similar to that of a general high school (Austrian children start high school at age 10,) and then again it's quite different. The classes are small – there are often classes with only three or four students – and sometimes it happens that the photographers have their field day, when there is but a single active boy at the Augarten Palace for an entire school semester. Then the professors sit with this one boy, while usually they take care of three or four, or at special times as many as eight students in one class. The consequence is that they are able to make more rapid progress, and this, in turn, helps because part of the school year has to be sacrificed for tours. The public high school at which the boys must pass their exams doesn't pay any attention to the tour problem, except that they require tests only twice a year, e.g. at the end of every semester, rather than throughout the school year. The courses of study which the Vienna Choir Boys have to pass correspond exactly to that which every other child of their age has to pass.

Is it necessary to explain that it is far more agreeable to study in groups of three or five in a palace from which one can readily run outside? A Vienna Choir Boy studies much more carefree than do his counterparts outside in the city by virtue of the fact that the professors who teach at the Augarten Palace do indeed assign homework and give tests, but do not issue report cards. He doesn't have to perform in front of a teacher who decides about his performance every day, but rather works with his teacher to prepare for tests, rather than against him.

The situation looks quite different from the standpoint of the school principal; difficult and unnerving. Teachers must be found and scheduled in such a way as to permit them to teach at other schools, but still be available for the necessary hours at the Vienna Choir Boys. It must be made eminently clear to the professors that while they are fully responsible for the proper class preparation of the boys, they must approach their teaching in a gentle manner. Perhaps a boy has just returned from a long trip; perhaps he is preparing to sing a great "Mass," or maybe three boys are preparing to appear in "The Magic Flute." Nevertheless these problems are not quite as serious as an outsider might suspect. Had it not been proven already in scientific tests at an artistic high school and at the Kodaly school in Hungary, one might use the Augarten Palace school as proof for the fact that the continuing and serious musical occupation of children, contrary to diverting their attention from other subjects, makes them more receptive and gives them the possibility to better concentrate.

The Vienna Choir Boys' schooling has changed very basically over the past decades. From Vienna Choir Boys generation to Vienna Choir Boys generation it has become better and better suited to the boys. Initially, when the Vienna Choir Boys were first founded, there was no separate school, and later on it was started on a part time basis. With time one found ever more teachers and the space for teaching. Many former choir boys remember well the fact that the Augarten Palace had neither a gymnasium nor a chemistry

In the world famous "Golden Hall" of the "Musikverein" in Vienna.

The ceremony marking the beginning of a Choir Boy's career: handing him his first uniform.

*O*ne choir of the Vienna Choir Boys on the grand staircase at the Augarten Palace.

*C*hoir Boys and the picture of Emperor Maximilian I., the founder of the institution.

An important visit from Great Britain: H.R.H. Diana, Princess of Wales, and the Vienna Choir Boys.

*A*s a Viennese institution, the Vienna Choir Boys are part and parcel of the city's cultural landscape, as for instance in front of the Upper Belvedere of Prince Eugen of Savoy, and, on special occasions, at the Spanisch Riding School.

*I*n front of the Augarten Palace, the home of the Vienna Choir Boys.

lab, and hardly any physics or geography demo materials, but rather solely small, plain classrooms. There was never any music study in the morning: it was held only in the afternoon in the form of rehearsals. Everything is different today. There is a gym, a swimming pool, the most modern facilities, and music education. In the end effect a house choir master may well also be a teacher, and may well be able to explain the studies using music which will be rehearsed in the afternoon, as an example.

Everything has changed, and yet everything has remained in principle the way it was forty years ago. In the morning the Vienna Choir Boys members are school children, if they are at home in Vienna. No ordinary school children, but rather children outside the school which issues their report card, and this fact is clearly visible on that line of the report which says "deportment." The boys are held harmless where other children have to fear poor marks for rowdy behavior or lack of attentiveness.

As compensation they do have what public schools do not teach any longer: schooling in behavior. It is taught by the director himself. One discusses manners and a natural bearing. The boys also are told that a kiss on the hand is no outdated ceremony, but rather a very nice sign towards women. In spite of the fact that they are not educated in a foreign service school, the choir boys are regarded as sort of "ambassadors", who are called upon to sing the national anthem of a foreign country alongside their own, and who must know how to behave in diplomatic surroundings; and that with natural elegance ...

Around lunch time, the choir members are transformed from students into hungry boys. They are famous for their appetite. In the dining room one may again observe what is true also in the dormitory: it's the camaraderie, the fun one has in eating together which is so important. The worries which children present to their parents at home when they don't want to eat, simply don't exist at the choir. Tradition dictates also a prayer at table; no strict ceremony, but rather a brief moment for contemplation and thankfulness. The "gentlemen's table" – that's how the table at which the director eats with the choir masters and ofttimes also with a guest is called – there are very special, secret and extremely important conversations, or so one thinks as a choir boy. In actuality one talks about the choir which is on tour at that moment, about a concert from the previous evening, or about very ordinary things. Perhaps also about whether the one or the other soloist will soon not be able to sing any longer. The conversation at the "gentlemen's table" is no more weighty than that, but it does no harm to instill respect in the boys for the "table." That, too, is part of proper manners.

After lunch there is time available for play outdoors, weather permitting. In the fenced-in area around the Augarten Palace, under tall old trees, on a manicured lawn, in the fresh air. There is only one limitation on the choir boys, compared to other boys of their age: they may not yell or play so hectically as to invite a cold later on.

Sometimes, during play time rarely, but during studies, during meals and on tour more frequently, the boys must observe "silencium" – silence. This means that until the order is cancelled, everyone must stop talking. Not a sound. One may not understand this as punishment and it may not be used as such. However, when a choir master orders "silencium" it simply means that the boys are to concentrate and guard their voices, that general silence must reign in order to make some sensitive situation more easily manageable. The "silencium," which is never used as a threat, is a specialty of the house to which the Vienna Choir Boys quickly adjust. It appears to be of benefit in later life as well. One learns and understands that it is often of advantage to keep ones mouth shut. One saves both ones voice and nerves. The daily rehearsal follows the play period, which, due to the necessary limitation on noise, hardly reminds one of the fact that there are boys at play. Rehearsals are held separately for each choir and according to ancient rules. First of all, the choir master must keep his choir in shape through vocalizing exercises, and make sure that no sloppiness creeps in. Secondly he must prepare the mass for the next Sunday as well as the repertory for the next tour. That requires planning and clear dispositions. The boys hardly notice anything about that. They rehearse for two hours, and these are rather fun with a choir master who understands how to spread enthusiasm. The Institute's artistic director, who often appears to check, hears more than that. He not only hears the boys and their momentary level of performance; he also hears whether the choir master is working properly, whether he is able to master the tasks, and whether one may send him off on a tour.

Good choir masters are a rare breed. In the ideal case they represent a mixture of choir pedagogue and creative musician. Once on tour, they are the final artistic judge on whom depends the tour's success, and they must prove themselves in front of these mercilessly critical boys day in day out. They must hear mistakes, correct pitch variations in acapella pieces through no more than a finger signal, sight read from score, and must be able to sing themselves. But beyond all that, they must relinquish all ego, and must dedicate the results of their labor to others. The masses sung at the Hofburg, the appearances of the Vienna Choir Boys in choral concerts or the opera: all these go under the sole title of "Vienna Choir Boys." Only that conductor is named who takes over the trained choir from its choir master for the final dress rehearsal, who adds the men's voices and instruments, and who then accepts the applause and the praise in the reviews. One surely knows which of the four choirs had sung and which choir master had prepared the choir. Some of these have become legends. However, to the outside world, at least in Vienna, it is the guest conductors who steal the limelight.

That ego suppression goes even further. Every choir master has taken the conducting course at the Conservatory with the hope of being allowed to stand up in front of an orchestra some day and of harvesting the stormy applause. Then all of a sudden he stands in front of a boys' choir, which is able only to provide him with a relative forte, and which, in spite of all the nuances and musicality, never offers to the conductor the feeling of power. It is therefore the characteristic of a good choir master of the Vienna Choir Boys, that he recognizes how much one can learn from working with boys' voices, that he can be retiring for a while, that he understands his steady presence with renowned musicians in concert halls and opera houses as learning experiences; that he thinks about how much he can learn on tour: not only the joy of applause, but also the art of organization and improvisation.

The Vienna Choir Boys have had many conductors in past years. That might lead one to the conclusion that each of them was able to stand it for no more than a year. However, one must calculate a bit differently, taking into consideration the fact that for years there have existed four choirs simultaneously, and that conductors are also needed for the preparatory courses and the student choir, which previously was called the reserve choir. A quick recalculation shows that the average length of a conductor's stay is significantly longer, and one can understand how many conductors the Institute "uses up." Some of them were choir boys themselves, and they are especially welcome at the Institute. Many of them have stayed true to their profession over the years, and one hardly notices the fact that there is no choir of any reputation in Vienna these days which is not firmly in the hands of a former Vienna Choir Boy. Every successful choir master has either been a Vienna choir boy himself, or has at least worked as a choir master for a few years. All important choral societies, such as the State Opera Chorus, the Society of the Friends of Music, the Musical Youth of Austria, etc, and all of those which are made up of amateurs, are taught and led by former members of the Vienna Choir Boys. The practice, as one may clearly see, has paid off for all of them.

Following the great personalities of the pioneering time, the renowned Ferdinand Grossmann and his successor Hans Gillesberger, we now have a music director who came from among the choir boys themselves, Uwe Harrer. He has worked for so long in the Augarten and the Hofburg that there is no doubt about his required experience, aside from all of his other excellent qualities.

The artistic director, the choir masters and the boys: they are all united daily for the two hours of rehearsal time. Soloist may also have their own practice sessions as needed. The work rhythm is never interrupted, and therefore the professional level of performance of the Vienna Choir Boys may be explained by this simple rule: practice, practice, practice.

The daily routine in Vienna is not especially sensational. School work is carried on under the word "silence." In between the boys must take lessons in at least one instrument, according to a complicated schedule. Many of them learn two instruments. They all require sound proof rooms both for their lessons and for instrumental practice. There is music everywhere at the Institute, and mostly at several places simultaneously. If one can name a place in Vienna where there is music every day and at every hour, then it surely must be the Augarten Palace. This statement is made after a thorough study of the operations of the opera houses, and the rehearsal schedules everywhere. As much music as is practiced at the Vienna Choir Boys exists nowhere else in the city of Vienna; in the Augarten Palace, the „Josefstöckl" next door, and in the surrounding houses which a former choir boy has built for today's choir boys: music is heard from everywhere.

The choir boys' day ends once again with free time, then dinner, and prior to lights out on those quiet days when they stay home, a bit of entertainment which is programmed by the prefect, and then the day is at an end. The prefects, in the ideal case again former choir members who return to the Institute during the time of their studies at the university, have their own recipe for quieting a choir down. Some of them tell tales of adventures which they had allegedly survived, others allow the boys to tell stories, some of them read to the boys. Only seldom does one find a pillow fight in progress in the dorm. They are a favorite scene for movie producers making a film about the Vienna Choir Boys, and they are at times posed for photographers. In reality, something which is seldom as fascinating as a movie, the boys just go to sleep.

Allgemeines Intelligenzblatt
zur Oesterreichisch = Kaiserlichen privil. Wiener = Zeitung.

145.   Montag, den 28. Junius   1830.

Concurs zu Plätzen für Hofsängerknaben im k. k. Convicte.

Da in der k. k. Hofmusik=Capelle Sängerknabenplätze zu besetzen sind, so haben diejenigen, welche einen derselben zu erhalten wünschen, bey dem am 9. August l. J. im k. k. Convicte am Universitätsplatze Nr. 796 abzuhaltenden Concurse zu erscheinen, in der Zwischenzeit aber sich bey dem Herrn Convicts=Director zur Vormerkung bey Zeiten anzumelden, und zugleich ihren Taufschein, ihre ärztlichen Zeugnisse über Schutzpocken=Impfung oder überstandene natürliche Blattern, dann die Zeugnisse ihrer Studien des letzten Semesters mitzubringen, bey welcher Gelegenheit über jeden sich meldenden Knaben eine Vorprüfung im Gesang vorgenommen wird, wozu jeder Mittwoch Nachmittag bestimmt ist. Die Concurrenten dürfen nicht unter 10 und nicht über 12 Jahre alt seyn, sie müssen die dritte Normal=Classe zurückgelegt haben, eine gute Stimme besitzen, im Fundamente des Gesanges so gut unterrichtet seyn, daß sie vom Blatte lesen, und fähig seyn, in die erste Grammatical=Classe einzutreten. Wenn der aufgenommene Knabe sich in Sitten und Studien auszeichnet, so hat er der Allerhöchsten Anordnung gemäß, auch nach Mutirung der Stimme im k. k. Convicte zu verbleiben; widrigen Falls aber nach dieser Mutirung, oder auch, wenn er im Gesang aus Mangel an Fähigkeit oder fleißiger Verwendung nicht die gehörigen Fortschritte machen sollte, auszutreten.

Von dem k. k. Hofmusikgrafen = Amte.

Wien den 21. Junius 1830.

Intell.Bl. 1830. Nr.145.

Already in 1830, a free position for a Choir Boy was announced in the daily newspaper – just as it is today.

Quite a contrast is the daily routine on tour, if you want to discuss sensation and excitement. Nevertheless the rules which apply are not too much different from those we have already described. Enough sleep and taking care of the voice. Without these two rules one cannot imagine a traveling day either in Australia or the U.S.A. The Vienna Choir Boys who practice the utmost routine, especially on tour, have never deviated from the axiom that the boys must ascend the podium well rested and with a well rested voice as well. If one follows these rules, hardly anything can go wrong.

The travel diaries which Rector Schnitt kept and the reports which prefects sent back home many years later, hardly differentiate themselves one from the other. Only the reorganization after Rector Schnitt's death, with its new contracts and new facilities such as airplanes, the ability to telephone throughout the world, and general comfort level increase has brought changes to the recounting following a tour by the Vienna Choir Boys. One has not changed anything about the principle; one has just conformed to today's realities.

The tours which the Vienna Choir Boys undertook during the legendary early times and even just after World War II, often lasted a long time and were very wearing, even if the boys didn't notice too much of that themselves. Today's tours are much more tightly organized, with new contracts negotiated with regional managers, and they last no longer than three to four months. Even the New Yorkers, who most cherish hearing the Vienna Choir Boys around Christmas time, must tolerate the fact that they arrive for their visit several days after the holidays. On Christmas eve, the Vienna Choir Boys can now be found at home. Tours in earlier times usually began with a long train trip followed by an adventuresome ocean crossing on a large liner, and then in the main excessively long trips on trains and rented buses. "The train trip was really quite nice: the boys were able to sleep lying down and even we still had room." So noted Rector Schnitt in 1932 on his way to America. "We still have two concerts and about 1300 miles till New York. If we include them, we can arrive at the following figures thus far: total distance about 23,630 km; number of concerts 61; of these 8 without opera. Audience about 103,000." This was noticed by a prefect in his diary in 1949. But the America tour was by no means coming to a close, the boys were still to be under way until April 1950. The ecclesiastic and his prefects traveled "the old fashioned way." This included the arrival in New York by ship, of course, gliding past the Statue of Liberty and the ocean steamers berthed at their piers which tooted their salute. Then one got the huge cooking pots out of a storage depot, which Rector Schnitt had rented in the thirties. This depot — uninformed people believed that the good Rector had gold bullion on deposit in this huge storage room — was the repository of kitchen utensils, unbreakable plates etc; i.e. a mobile kitchen which then went along for the trip throughout the states. On those days when the Vienna Choir Boys were not invited at an artistic or political club, an association of Austrians or a religious order, the cooking was done in the hotel, both because it was cheaper and because the boys should have home cooking on such long trips. They should be able to eat roast pork with kraut and dumplings even when they are thousands of kilometers from home. But this also meant that Rector Schnitt or his delegate went looking for a jewish delicatessen right after the choir's arrival, for only there could one obtain the ingredients for a european meal, and also the sorely missed black bread.

He who thinks that touring in prior times took place in a gypsy atmosphere could hardly be contradicted. The constant switching back and forth between opulent appearances and improvisation — the prohibited cooking in hotels, the interminable bus trips through the American continent, the exciting adventures with those large costume wardrobes which were suddenly missing from the train, the quick change of scenery — all this kept the boys and their accompanying personnel much more out of breath than do the well organized tours today, when airplanes take care of travel quickly and in comfort. In the Scandinavian countries it was quite normal for substitute parents to fetch the boys from the train at every stop, so that they could spend nearly every day getting spoiled by their hosts. All this the management has tried to curtail somewhat: the close contact with philanthropists and friends, as for example those in Sweden who spoil "their" choir boys, who come to visit them in Vienna and who keep track of them for many years – but it is impossible to stop it over night.

Nevertheless more rest is indicated: they are not to take wild bus tours between their arrival in a city and their evening appearance, but rather are to lie down to sleep.

Have the choir's travels lost something of their sensation, their flair because of this? Certainly not – they are not any less exciting for today's active boys than they were for earlier generations; they are still an adventure.

The daily routine on tour, after the long journey or flight is behind them and the other continent or the British Isles has been reached, follows the same guide lines we have mentioned ofttimes before. Vienna Choir Boys must get enough sleep and may not become hoarse. If on the morning after a concert there is no possibility of an extended sleep, then the boys must sleep on the train, bus or airplane, or must make it up the next afternoon at the hotel. If hosts offer cold drinks just prior to a concert, they must be declined with thanks. Should time, space, or climate change cause nervousness, then "silence" must restore peace and quiet.

Rehearsals on tour are reduced to a minimum. The choirs usually have worked ahead either in Vienna or in their vacation spot, so that the tour program can hardly be made more perfect. It occasionally is necessary to correct small sloppinesses or to get accustomed to the special acoustics of a new auditorium. But no matter what, one always has to vocalize before every concert. Tapes which are sent back to Vienna report on the choir's progress and show the people back home whether the performance level is being maintained. In some cases the music director may have to make a quick two day trip to England or a week's trip to South America, if a choir displays signs of tiredness and has to be brought up to snuff prior to an important concert. In earlier times the boys, their prefect and nurse remained virtually without contact with home for long periods of time. Now they feel close to the Institute no matter where in the world they are. That is not to say that control is the most important thing, but rather the secure feeling which a choir master gets, because help can be on the way quickly.

Even in the time shortly after World War II, a choir and its young choir master were away from Vienna for half a year, and so any dereliction of his duties could have been disastrous for the Vienna Choir Boys' reputation over time. Today that's no longer thinkable. One no longer performs without a "net."

Since rehearsals on tour are kept to a minimum, the boys have time to engage in social activities. Their evening concerts bring the great, adoring public and the critics, but also the financial means for the Vienna Institute. Invitations to visit clubs, heads of state, receptions which are given by Austria's diplomatic representatives are by no means exclusively meant to provide entertainment for the boys. They are required of every group which beats the drum for Austria in one way or another. That means that every Vienna choir boy while on tour, "stands on stage" from morning till late, whether in leisure clothes on the bus or in uniform on airplanes. Even an appearance in a hotel lobby is not a minor affair. Passers-by in Tokyo are astounded by the boys' excellent deportment; Australian journalists are not interested only in the boys' musical abilities, but also in their daily menu. Interviews must be granted, photographers are ever nearby, and even a visit to the zoo or other local tourist attractions mean an official appearance of the Vienna Choir Boys.

Fortunately all this is not constantly in the boys' consciousness. They are amused by gorillas, are astounded by sky scrapers, genuinely enjoy seeing real cowboys, and love it when one receives them with Japanese manners.

Their ability to absorb impressions is enormous, as is their capacity for ice cream and movies, as may be gleaned from a reading of their diaries. The fact that they themselves are a sensation is of lesser importance to them, than the fact that they experience sensations daily. They quickly form friendships with their surrogate parents and have no problem in their contacts with their hosts. They always display the good behavior which they were taught at home at the Augarten Palace. Nevertheless, they have no illusions and are not affected in their behavior. A touring choir has always consisted of twenty to twenty four boys, and never of „Wunderkinder." No choir has ever disappointed the Vienna Choir Boys' friends around the world, and no tour has ever been a disappointment for them. In the life of every Vienna Choir Boy there will be at least one big tour to far-away lands, and one which will take them to performances in their own country. Only at a later time when a choir boy no longer sings, will the difference between these two kinds of trips become clear to him. As long as he is active, he has no time to think or to be conceited; he will like New York, Tokyo or Salzburg equally well.

At the center of a tour day there always is the concert. It usually takes place in a theater, a concert hall, or more rarely in a church. The touring choir normally carries along two programs for concert halls as well as a varied one for church concerts in their baggage. The boys' find their variety not so much in the changing program, but rather in the ever changing conditions under which the concerts take place, and in the public acceptance which is always a surprise. At one time they cheer a presentation of motets, then wait again until they are enthused by the concluding waltz. The greatly varied concert halls are enough to prevent a routine from grabbing hold on tour: one time there are crowded dressing rooms in which one hardly can dress for an opera; another time the curtain doesn't work or the piano is tuned at the very last minute. Sometimes a local manager has taken it upon himself to change the program on his own, and the choir master finds out about it just as the concert starts. Sometimes the prefect, who among his duties must also push scenery around and take charge of costuming, has a merry-go-round, which he has assembled with great difficulty, collapse on him, and the boys on stage must improvise. It often happens that especially in operettas or acted-out operas, for reasons of space, the piano must be placed in such a way that the choir master doesn't see the boys or prevents the boys from being able to see him out of the corners of their eyes. Then it's a matter of fixing mistakes between the boys and the piano by means of invented passages or an improvised scene.

In barely two hours the Vienna Choir Boys must prove evening after evening that they are able to keep up their standards, singing a great variety of music from the songs of the Renaissance to the music of Jacques Offenbach, Schubert or Johann Strauss, and even contemporary composers, and all that without competition.

He who thinks that the boys are subject to the pressure of success forget that these are boys. They are only rarely aware of how difficult their artistry is, and they are only rarely told how hard it is. Only in retrospect, as former Vienna Choir Boys, do they become aware of how much they had to do and how much they knew.

Above all, they must keep a very select audience at breathless attention. While there have not been any in depth studies, one is able to say, based on experience and conversation with experts, that it ist usually the experts and music lovers who attend Vienna Choir Boys concerts. They often arrive with preconceived notions – not always with the best ones! One has to prove to them right in the first part of the concert, with ecclesiastic works and new music, that the Vienna Choir Boys are the true preservers of the tradition of the Hofmusikkapelle. In countries with their own great choral tradition, as for instance in Great Britain, the number of genuine music experts present at a Vienna Choir Boys concert is usually quite high, and the success is quite tremendous even before the first intermission.

For another part of the audience in all the world, the Vienna Choir Boys conjure up a picture of a former homeland. The century of the great wars, and emigraton have caused many Austrians to settle all over the world: Austrians who are not necessarily all music lovers, but who nevertheless don't want to miss a concert by the Vienna Choir Boys, and often travel great distances in order to be there in Milwaukee or elsewhere and to be moved secretly or openly when a Schubert choral work is sung. It matters not that the former home of these overseas Austrians has changed so very much, that for many of them it would not be recognizable any longer. The Vienna Choir Boys bring with the masters of Viennese music a picture of the homeland which has remained unchanged and in its own way has remained true. One should pay attention to those awakened memories and moving experiences.

A large part of the audience at concerts of the Vienna Choir Boys, likely the greatest percentage, consists of women of all ages who come to watch and listen to the singing boys. They are not among the most critical listeners, and they applaud especially quickly. They likely are most enamored of the operas and operettas in the middle part of the concert, when the boys are in costume, when they sing and act, run hither and yon across the stage with crinoline and wigs singing Mozart, Offenbach or Strauss. It would be silly to criticize this part of the audience for coming to the Vienna Choir Boys' concert for the sheer entertainment of it. It would appear to be much more important to note that this part of the audience will be raised to a much loftier cultural level, than would be the case with mothers's day songs and fashionable folk music. It is true that the mere existence of the choir consisting of twenty four well washed and simultaneously bowing boys many be enough of an occasion for some to buy a ticket of admission. But even they will then hear the music of Orlando di Lasso, Palestrina, Ernst Krenek, Robert Schumann, Johannes Brahms, and will find the works of these masters beautiful. Isn't that perfectly alright? Should one simply do without these people? Realists will take sufficient satisfaction in the financial consideration that one cannot do without them. To make it palatable for purists one must point up the disciplinary aspects of this work. And this education actually takes place when one considers that many pop fans end up applauding the works of Orlando di Lasso.

All of the programs of the Vienna Choir Boys conclude with a work based on a composition by either Johann Strauss Sr. or Jr. The only answer one can give to all those who might object to this, is that everyone throughout the world expects of Viennese musicians that they bring with them music from Vienna. The Vienna Philharmonic will likely not be invited because one wants to hear them play Berlioz, but one rather wants to hear their interpretation of Mozart, Schubert and Bruckner. The Vienna State Opera is expected to present works by Mozart, Richard Strauss and Alban Berg. Should it then only be the Vienna Choir Boys, who out of pride, should fail to present, at the end of their concerts, something which reminds the world of the fact, that the waltz was the last great art form which embarked upon its world wide, victorious travels from Vienna?

There are innumerable examples which show that the management of the Vienna Choir Boys has steadfastly declined demands on the part of concert managers, and has retained balanced and serious programs. Fortunately it can not be reported that the Vienna Choir Boys have ever been unworldly. One never has arranged programs which intentionally declined success. One never has undertaken tours which were designed exclusively to evoke critics' accolades. That audience which secures the existence of the Vienna Choir Boys through their enthusiasm and their money, has always been well served.

There always have been attempts to introduce contemporary music into the Vienna Choir Boys' concerts. One has gone on tour with an opera especially composed for the Vienna Choir Boys by Benjamin Britten; but the impresarios have spoken the last word and have declined "contemporary" works during negotiations for more favorable contracts.

That's the hard reality of it.

It is with this reality that the three accompanying people, who share the responsibility for the twenty-four boys, are confronted on tour. Choir master, prefect, and nurse. The choir master must conduct the concerts, must bear the concern for the evenness of the musical standards; must keep the voices in shape; and aside from all that must represent the City of Vienna at innumerable invitations, dinners after concerts, conferences with local managers and small talks with the chair persons of ladies' groups. The fact that he himself might just have completed college, and perhaps might not yet be a man of the world, is something which he may not allow to peek through. On the contrary, he must quickly become a man of the world.

The prefect must play his part. He, too, is responsible for the behavior and security of the boys. He decides, along with the choir master, when and how long the boys are to sleep. He assigns the choir to their respective hotel rooms. He makes sure that no personal luggage stays behind. He has the airline tickets, and he has the passports. He is often even younger than the choir master, and yet already a master at improvisation – especially a master at improvised sleeping on planes, on trains or on a bus when everything has been done and he knows that nothing can happen for the next two hours or so – and then has to have his sleep disturbed by twenty four boys who want to be entertained. He must see to it that the adoring audience does not advance to the dressing rooms before, during and after a concert. The boys must have their peace and quiet. He must never lose his temper, regardless of the circumstances, must always appear in control, to give the boys the needed sense of security which allows them to travel safely throughout the world. In the sixty years of Vienna Choir Boys' travels around the globe, there has hardly ever been an accident.

The nurse is usually, but not always, a motherly type of person. Her duties are as precisely delineated as are those of the two gentlemen. She sews tears in the costumes, uniforms and the leisure dress worn on tours. She soothes home sickness, colds, scraped knees. She washes necks. She doubles before a concert as costume lady and make-up artist. She is sometimes even a replacement mother. As is the case with the choir master and prefect, she may not have a favorite on a tour, but must see to it that each of the twenty-four boys gets the identical feeling of her concern.

The three adults who go along on tour maintain the contact with home. The choir master reports to the Institute; telephones if need be; sends tape recordings which provide information about the condition of the choir. Together with the prefect and the nurse he is the highest authority of the touring choir. The fact that all three are usually young people themselves, and that the choir master and prefect more often than not are former Choir Boys themselves, makes life with the boys that much easier. At every moment there is something exciting happening, and the children's attention is focused on so many new impressions, that they hardly ever have time to consider that travel could be strenuous.

After a concert by the Vienna Choir Boys overseas, the diplomatic representatives of Austria often find it easier to form contacts and to present the desires of their country. That is why journalists have given the Vienna Choir Boys the moniker "Singing Ambassadors of Austria". The travels of the Vienna Choir Boys, by contrast to other cultural institutions' overseas travels, are not subsidized. On the contrary, they are undertaken in order to bring in the money which assures the Choir's existence in Vienna.

The tours offer the boys experiences from which they profit for years to come. They learn to move about securely and in a relaxed fashion in ever new and often exotic environments. They get to know how one lives in large, fancy hotels. They lose all timiditiy before crowned heads. They make contact with peoples all over the world. They get to pick up language fragments everywhere. They get to know areas and cities of the world, of which other boys their age may only dream. They have friends everywhere. They work with musicians of world renown. They get to know in a most natural way the repertoires of opera houses and concert halls. If one sometimes wonders about the

*E*very Sunday morning in Vienna I, Hofburg: after celebration of mass.

*D*uring performances and rehearsals under their artistic director Uwe Chr. Harrer.

*R*ecordingsessions for records and broadcasts are part of every Vienna Choir Boy's routine.

*M*ake-up and standing by for "The Magic Flute" at the Vienna State Opera.

*F*or many years the three boys in Mozart's "The Magic Flute" have been supplied by the Vienna Choir Boys.

*N*o performance of "Carmen" at the Vienna State Opera has been able to do without the Vienna Choir Boys: such as Franco Zeffirelli's shown here. Their conductors, in the course of time, have been Lorin Maazel, Carlos Kleiber, Herbert von Karajan and many others.

*F*or viewers in Vienna and for the entire Austrian Television, the Lead soloist in Gian Carlo Menotti's "Amahl and the Night Visitors" naturally was a Vienna Choir Boy.

*A*gain and again: the life of a Choir Boy consists of all sorts of things,
but above all of a great deal of music study.

*I*n their hands lay, and still lies, the fate of the Vienna Choir Boys: it was Monsignore Josef Schnitt who re-founded the Choir after World War I. Hofrat Walter Tautschnig was the head of the Institute from 1955 to 1983. Today Hofrat Tautschnig is still the President of the Society "Vienna Choir Boys". His son, Dr. Walter Tautschnig, became the Choir's director in 1983.

*T*he President: Walter Tautschnig sen.

*T*he Director: Walter Tautschnig jun.

*P*assing on the experience of a lifetime: Hofrat Walter Tautschnig during an intensive rehearsal.

In Jacques Offenbach's "Monsieur et Madame Denis", one of the solo players must act as a girl.

*F*un with Jacques Offenbach: the gaiety of his tunes inspires the boys in their costumes.

*D*ressed up in costumes, the Choir Boys are turned into singing little ladies and gentlemen.

fact that a Vienna Choir Boy doesn't bring home any earnings in the usual sense, one is apt to forget that he has gathered valuable experience for his later life. He learns to act independently, and to find his way in strange environments. It is a fact that it has been helpful for me to oversleep in New York as a Vienna Choir Boy, and then to have to find my way by taxi to the concert hall. That I learned to ask for the concert hall in Swedish cities; that I saw, however briefly, the beauty of Bruge and Ghent; that I met students on American college campuses; that I went along on a crossing on the "Queen Elizabeth", then the world's largest passenger liner; that I learned about the many people with other ways of life in other parts of the world. I certainly learned about worldliness and tolerance. The band-width of recollections is enormous. A former Vienna Choir Boy is at home anywhere in the world, but above all in music. In a concert he hears more clearly than almost any other visitor when a singer takes a breath at the wrong place, or a conductor loses contact with his orchestra. Is the time as a Vienna Choir Boy the ideal school for life? It most certainly is that. Anecdotes? In his memoirs, Rector Schnitt writes that he had never found the time to keep a diary. However, there are some writings from his own hand. Many prefects, in their reports to the Institute, note that there is an across the board gain of weight to be detected among the boys, or that there has been some humorous occurrence. All of the choir boys take photos, send home letters and postcards, and decades later still dig through their remembrances around the clock.

It is virtually impossible now to decide which of the papal audiences was the most exciting. Or which choir has the nicest memories of the USA. One really would have to allow those boys who were under way with Rector Schnitt to tell their own stories of how he cooked. One would have to tell the many stories of one or the other nurse, who without any special language knowledge was trying to impart the secrets of making „Wienerschnitzl" to a cook in distant Canada. One would have to tell how difficult sometimes the farewells from a distant continent could be. One should tell about the happy cloistered nuns who invited the Vienna Choir Boys to afternoon tea, or those nuns who one Christmas took in the choir in the vicinity of New York, and then had to note that all of the boys managed to garner a cowboy revolver aside from a sensible gift from Macy's.

A three or maximum four month long trip nowadays passes incredibly fast. The days are fully occupied with sight seeing, life at the hotel, the concerts, and the trip to the next city. The boys sleep well and without any complications. All of a sudden it's the next to the last concert, and in ones thoughts one may well be already in Vienna. In three days one will be again sitting in school. Will be singing in the Hofburgkapelle in two short weeks. There's a performance of "The Magic Flute" scheduled at the opera for next Saturday. Neither the real excitement nor the invented drama of a Vienna Choir Boys' trip has ever been set down in a film or a book. It would assuredly be most difficult to do so.

A Vienna Choir Boy's career ends almost as quickly as a tour. One suddenly realizes that one will shortly no longer be able to be a soprano, that one will be fourteen, and no longer able to appear at the opera, or the concert hall, or in Tokyo. That one will no longer be at home in front of microphones or in the spotlight; that the time will come to prepare for a career like every other fourteen year old, albeit with somewhat better chances, and also with a small debit: one already has a past. One leaves a childhood behind which was much more exciting and impressionable than that of any other fourteen year old.

Are there really no problems which stem from these circumstances? How much does a Vienna Choir Boy salvage from his childhood to take along into later life? Does one manage the transition into a normal life without any difficulties? That's another very interesting chapter.

The Imperial Choir Boys in 1809: good marks for Franz Schubert.

The Extraordinary, Ordinary Life

I

If one were to answer the question as to the success formula for the quality of the Vienna Choir Boys, one would give the following recommendation: take musically inclined children, educate them carefully, let them sing in the Hofburgkapelle – and this continually for at least five centuries, and you'll hardly have to worry about the Vienna Choir Boys' singing quality. But likely there is a second special attribute missing in other choral groups, even if they had the tradition. The re-founder of the Hofmusikkapelle and founder of the Vienna Choir Boys Institution, Josef Schnitt, was an ecclesiastic gentleman raised on a farm. He had a very special sense of tradition, including a sense of financial security for the present, and planning for the ever insecure future. Had he been a narrow minded idealist, he might only have had the laudable idea to let boys' voices resound again through the Hofburg and the past sixty years might have looked quite different. It would be incorrect to assume that the entire world, and therefore Vienna as well, exclusively loved and advanced the cause of the Vienna Choir Boys. Rector Schnitt loved his Choir Boys and planned for their secure future.

He was an energetic, attentive man of small stature, with all of the attributes which one imagines a founder to have. It makes little difference whether we are speaking of the founder of a philanthropic organization or the founder of a business. He had a wonderful way with children and also with others with whom he had to deal. Regardless of whether it was a diplomat or a farmer from eastern Tyrol: he always managed to find the proper tone, and more often than not, there was in the background something of a demand – a demand never for himself, but rather always for his boys. His negotiating partners rarely if ever managed to react in a negative way. Only in government offices did one manage to hold back. The battles which Rector Schnitt fought with the bureaucracy has indeed entered into the history of the Institute, but has hardly ever surfaced in public. He never even wrote very much about this in his book about the Vienna Choir Boys.

He was constantly on the lookout for donors and sponsors for the Vienna Choir Boys, but at the same time made it quite clear that these donors could take no influence on the Institute which he managed. He never relinquished his responsibilities, neither before nor after World War II. He personally retained control over every detail, from the conclusion of contracts about world tours to the decision concerning the purchase of materials for costumes. He was ever the sole manager in all questions concerning the Vienna Choir Boys.

It's no wonder that legends arose around him even during his lifetime. He had many friends but also some opponents. He found his friends everywhere, and some of his enemies wherever an attempt was made to exercise influence on his Institute. To his boys, the countless Choir Boys who went to his school, he was an idol for life. If one were to ask them today to draw up a picture of Rector Schnitt, all of them would remember two incidents during their Vienna Choir Boys existence: one might be a joke they played on the Tector, after which they were honestly afraid of him, and the other was a Sunday evening when their parents brought them to the Institute and Rector Schnitt received them with a smile, a gentle stroke through their hair and the words: "My boy". This was an honor which he bestowed without any recognizable occasion. No choir boy could ever report how one could have earned this "my boy". It was simply a present.

Rector Schnitt was really quite the opposite of the traditional manager in all of his undertakings. He dealt with the shopkeepers and the farmers who supplied his "Vienna Choir Boys Hotel" in Hinterbichl in a very special way; usually with a handshake.

Sometimes they got the better of him; then again he had a stroke of luck and had the advantage over them. But the dignity of his ecclesiastic position and his healthy sense for the preservation of property seldom led to failure. It must be borne in mind that to found the Vienna Choir Boys he put up his personal assets. Even the church had little influence on Rector Schnitt. He bowed reverently before the popes who received his boys, and he was a faithful servant of his church. But had the church made demands on him to direct the Vienna Choir Boys into this or that direction, he would have turned them down flat. They were *his* choir boys.

When he died, he left an Institute which he had led through decades of hard time, and which enjoyed an excellent reputation throughout the world. It was clear to him that the Institute had to be upgraded to the new era. Some of the changes he still approved, but did not himself initiate anymore. He approved the formation of the Association of the Vienna Choir Boys which assures that there never would be any outside influence. Since he was a man of God, he had faith in his Lord, and was quite sure that He helped the Vienna Choir Boys again and again.

The initiation of the significant changes in the organization of the Vienna Choir Boys, which had to be made after Rector Schnitt's death, fell on the shoulders of Hofrat Dr. Tautschnig. Tautschnig was the right man for the job, as a former Vienna Choir Boy of the first generation and later a prefect, then as a member of the state government of Carynthia, and as a member of the Association of the Vienna Choir Boys and advisor to Rector Schnitt during his last years. Immediately upon Rector Schnitt's death he asked Ferdinand Grossmann to take over the artistic directorate at the Augarten Palace. He wanted to make sure that the musical future of the Vienna Choir Boys was in competent hands. Every former Vienna Choir Boy remains for the rest of his life an expert in matters Vienna Choir Boys. Tautschnig did not want to have that sole responsibility in artistic questions. He renegotiated the contracts and insisted that the choirs get a more just share of the tour profits. He cancelled the unusually long travels, and made more effective use of his choirs through the use of airplanes and modern organizational means. He tried to reduce the improvised nature of the choirs' activities and to build greater security into every activity. Above all he sold the vacation village including the "Vienna Choir Boys Hotel" in Hinterbichl, something which Rector Schnitt had decided, but was unable to effect during his lifetime. He built instead a new vacation spot on the Lake Wörthersee, and this resulted in a significant change in the life of the Vienna Choir Boys.

These minor and major tasks were joined by a personal one: Dr. Tautschnig had to establish himself on Vienna's musical scene, something which is not without its intrigues. He had to make clear to all of the contractual partners that he now would make all of the decisions with regard to the Vienna Choir Boys. He had to convince them that while the Association of the Vienna Choir Boys had the ultimate responsibility, an Institute of this size and with the complexities of tasks had to be managed from a single desk.

During this phase of the reorganization of the Vienna Choir Boys, it is not surprising that problems arose. Suddenly there were boys from Vienna singing overseas, who were certainly not the Vienna Choir Boys. This sort of thing always happens when an institution has become so famous, that the mere similarity with its competitive organization is enough to assure success. Tautschnig was able to handle this problem. The Vienna Choir Boys remained unassailable, and the result of many discussions and law suits was the confirmation that the Vienna Choir Boys, who sing in the Hofmusikkapelle, are the sole successors to the famous Hofsängerknaben.

Tautschnig's success is higly visible and also understandable. He appeared at the right time a new style. He allowed the founding years to be followed by years of healthy, careful expansion. Nevertheless he did not allow the inner structure of the Vienna Choir Boys to be changed as a result of measures he undertook on a business level. Quite to the contrary, he placed the artistic dignity of Vienna Choir Boys into the foreground. He slimmed down the Vienna Choir Boys' activities: they no longer sing operettas in Vienna; they are not to be had for advertising; and during recording sessions it is their artistic excellence which is paramount.

Hofrat Tautschnig has cleared the way for his son. Dr. Walter Tautschnig is now the Director. He has the previously mentioned prerequisites, was also a Vienna Choir Boy, knows the Institute as well as his family does, and represents once again a new generation with all of the novelties of the outgoing twentieth century, from the computer to modern management techniques. Nevertheless, that which one may call the conscience of the institution, has hardly changed at all. The old fashioned concepts of discipline, tradition, and order still have their validity, and it would be wrong to deprecate that fact. That might sound reactionary, but is meant honestly and should be properly understood by everyone.

2. Juni 1972.

Sehr geehrter Herr Hofrat,

Darf ich, nach London zurück-gekehrt, noch einmal herzlich danken für die Zeit, die Sie mir und meinen Freunden geschenkt haben und für den unvergeßlichen Eindruck der Stimmen Ihrer Zöglinge. Ich habe sie am Sonntag in der Hofkapelle noch einmal gehört und höre Sie noch in der Erinnerung.

Als Erzieherin und Kinderpsychologin war ich auch nicht weniger beeindruckt von der pädagogischen und menschlichen Seite Ihrer Arbeit, ganz abgesehen von der Schönheit der Umgebung, in der die Kinder aufwachsen.

Mit Respekt und Bewunderung,

Ihre Anna Freud

Anna Freud about the correct education of a Vienna Choir Boy.

II

Even Vienna Choir Boys go on vacation: to relax and to prepare for the life of a choir boy. Until the sixties, vacation was inimitably linked with Hinterbichl, Hinterbichl in East Tyrol at the foot of the Grossvenediger mountain. A tiny village with but a few farm houses and the property of the Vienna Choir Boys. Rector Schnitt discovered the area on a mountain climb, and then converted it with a great deal of personal effort into a vacation spot. At first the boys were put up with farmers. Then they got their own house, and then a hotel with all of the necessary additions such as a "Kaffeehaus", a butcher shop, and its own hydroelectric powerhouse to supply the necessary current. Hinterbichl was built over a period of decades – and was never finished.

Rector Schnitt was convinced that Hinterbichl solved numerous problems simultaneously. Budding choir boys first came to spend their vacation in East Tyrol and there found the much needed friendships in the choir. They climbed mountains and forgot all about being homesick. They were very satisfied in the fresh air and with food nourishment. They prepared for their very first trip.

The active choir boys stayed in training and were not disrupted, since they spent their vacation within the framework of the Institute.

Former Vienna Choir Boys also came to Hinterbichl. They were helpful in many functions of the "Vienna Choir Boys Hotel", and spent an enjoyable summer as waiters, as apprentices in the butchery and at other activities. The guests who were enticed to come from around the world were supposed to maintain good contacts with the Institute, to relax and to help finance the vacation spot.

Things almost went well. Only the financial calculation was incorrect and Hinterbichl did not become a source of income for the Institute. Times changed, the tourist demands escalated, and finally there was nothing that

Hinterbichl had to offer that they could not get elsewhere. And the boys, especially the active choir boys were squeezed together into rather primitive sleeping accommodations. The kids hardly noticed this at all. After all it was rather fun living a spartan existence during the summer. The former choir boys were satisfied with Hinterbichl in view of the fact that they spent their early lives there, when they were children, and now could feel almost like adults. Faithful guests were satisfied even without a private bath. But nobody could really be truly satisfied.

Hinterbichl naturally means a great deal more for a former Vienna choir boy: it is a reminiscence of a happy childhood, of building castles, of whittling ships from tree bark, or climbing the Grossvenediger. He remembers Hinterbichl as being connected with the time when his voice changed, with his first love, with the first time he earned some money, with a whole raft of wonderful summers. The memories of Hinterbichl are laced with visions of Rector Schnitt coming from the butcher shop with his sleeves rolled up. He supervised the kitchen. He read mass on Sundays. A coffee machine blew up right under his nose. He often called choir boys and those whose voices have changed "my boy". He treats rather grown-up guests, former choir boys, in his tyrannical style, and puts the fear of God into successful businessmen. One thinks the Rector is coming, and for a moment one reverts to being a choir boy. Always in his cassock, small, watchful, the founder and nourisher of every Vienna Choir Boy. He was never so much in his element as he was in Hinterbichl.

But even during his lifetime it seemed obvious that Hinterbichl would some day have to become a tourist place without Vienna Choir Boys. He asked his later successor to look for a replacement for Hinterbichl. The fact that it was only found after his death, and therefore became one of the features of the Vienna Choir Boys' new era, was only right. The new spot, Sekirn on Lake Wörthersee, would surely habe pleased Rector Schnitt. But it is good that he did not live to see the end of Hinterbichl. After all, it was *his* Hinterbichl.

The Vienna Choir Boys, originally city boys, by all means should spend their summers in the open air. They should live together and be able to practice now and then. If possible, they should not go on vacation with their parents, because the sense of togetherness becomes a fact where differences are obliterated. Worried parents, however, might reawaken those differences. Hinterbichl was ideally situated: far away from Vienna. There was hardly room there for parents.

Today the Vienna Choir Boys are no longer solely city kids. The fact that they are able to vacation without the public being present is very positive. Being in the spotlight all year long requires quiet and undisturbed vacation, even if there's a little rehearsing now and then. Sekirn, the current synonym for choir boys vacation, is located on Lake Wörthersee and encompasses an enormous amount of land: half a mountain and an entire forest are included. In prior times one was of the opinion that proximity to the mountains was of climatic advantage for the boys. Now one has chosen the sunniest, most rain-free area of Austria. Vacationers from all over the world pay good money to come to Carinthia. The location is ideal. One is only minutes away from a larger city – Klagenfurt, with its airport and excellent train connections. In spite of this, the Vienna Choir Boys' property is peaceful and quiet. The only noise which is allowed comes from happy boys themselves. A stone garden was planted with edelweiss and gentian to remind one of Hinterbichl.

The vacation home is very spacious and utilitarian. All four choirs may be there at the same time, should the need arise. Each of them has its own dormitory, its own wash rooms, own showers, many large rehearsal rooms, dining rooms, and the sun shines constantly. There's also a very large "family room" which can be used for concerts, and which allows the boys to play indoors during inclement weather – rarely.

There's also a private hospital which is mostly empty, but it is good to be prepared for any and all eventuality. A fireplace under a roof in front of the building permits apples to be baked. There's table tennis and the Vienna Choir

Boys' favorite sport, soccer. The boys also have a private landing on the lake for swimming.

Gone are the times when the choirs slept adjacent to the hotel which bore their name. Now they are the center of attraction. Everything is focused on nothing but their needs and their relaxation and rest.

But there's work even in Sekirn. While the active choirs are still on tour, the "eleves", the former reserve choir, the ones who are training to become Vienna Choir Boys, practice. If there's enough space, then former Choir Boys are invited. When the active choirs come to Sekirn, the noise level increases somewhat. New costumes are made in the costume shop and Hofrat Tautschnig makes good use of his experience and coaches a new operetta as director. On weekends there's singing in a small chapel. The kitchen is charged with preparing huge portions to satisfy the enormous Vienna Choir Boys appetite. The entire house rings with singing and laughter. Sometimes there's a sort of sample concert for which it is not difficult at all to obtain an audience. Afterwards the boys are alone again and have their peace. The ones who were "eleves" for a summer in Sekirn and who passed their probation period in Vienna, are handed their uniforms, and finally become Vienna Choir Boys.

Wiener Sängerknaben

EHEMALS K.K. HOFSÄNGERKNABEN · GEGRÜNDET 1498

III

There's planning for both vacation time and for the time after the voice changes. The special circumstances are considered and plans are made well in advance. Former Vienna Choir Boys don't become normal fifteen year-old from one day to the next, but rather remain for a time, above all as former Vienna Choir Boys, true to the Institute and its special life style and just a little bit different from other children.

What happens when a change of singing register no longer helps? When one has to go out "into life" as a result of completion of the fourth high school grade? What happens in this "terrible" situation of leave taking?

There was a time honored tradition that the choir boys of the Hofmusik-kapelle were taken care of even after their voices changed (the mutants). But another tradition has come about for the Vienna Choir Boys: a former choir boy may live, even later on, in the "Mutantenhaus", to live on in the circle of the Vienna Choir Boys, to search for and to find a quiet transition. Rector Schnitt had already adapted the "Josefstöckl", a small building a stone's throw from the Augarten Palace, for the mutants. In the course of the years, Hofrat Tautschnig had four houses built on the perimeter of the Augarten Palace. They provide rooms not only for many functions of the Institute but also for the mutants. Ex-Vienna Choir Boys now live in two of the houses. They will forever remain Vienna Choir Boys.

The choir boys point with pride at their ex-choir boys who have graduated from high school. While they went through the first four years in an accelerated tempo and under extraordinary conditions, it is good to know that they fitted well into their regular classes.

Nevertheless there exists a threshold. There are also problems one should not deny. Practice has shown that former Vienna Choir Boys must learn to live a different lifestyle. They must get accustomed to the fact that they are tested and observed throughout the school year; that their intimate knowl-

edge of the habits of far away countries is highly valued, but that the knowledge of grammar in a foreign language is more important for good grades.
Meeting a head of state or the Holy Father remains only as a memory.

There have been cases – they are rare but they exist – when a Choir Boy
is not immediately able to find his way back into the reality of the life of a normal fifteen-year-old. But in general they are strong enough to be able to
manage the transition. One may come to the Hofburgkapelle on Sundays.
One is still always welcome at the Augarten Palace. After a short time one can
again begin to sing; now in the Choralschola or in the Chorus Viennensis,
which also concertizes and makes recordings together with the Vienna Choir
Boys. One eventually begins to live ones own life, but still remains near ones
childhood.

There are a number of famous musicians who once were Vienna Choir Boys:
Ludwig Senfl, Jacobus Gallus, Franz Schubert, Carl Zeller, as a "substitute"
Joseph Haydn, the conductors Felix Mottl, Carl Richter, Clemens Krauss and
Lovro von Matacic. From the many generations of Vienna Choir Boys since
1924 there have evolved some notable musicians but none of international
fame. The Vienna Choir Boys supply personnel to many of the musical organizations of their native city Vienna. The Vienna Philharmonic Orchestra, the
Vienna Symphony Orchestra, the choir of the Vienna State Opera, and to
many of the important choral organizations. One also finds them again conducting in the pits of the houses at the state level. They are all good musicians
who are proud of their childhood. They have a very special ear for singing.
They know just the right tempo for the Viennese classics. They grew up in an
unbroken tradition. In spite of the fact that one seldom reads their names on
large billboards, they are nevertheless important personalities. Taken alto-
gether they form the basis for all of the musical activities which give rise to
the moniker "Vienna, city of music." That's because that basis is made up of
the orchestras, choruses and music teachers.

The predominant number of former Choir Boys goes into professional life.

They become doctors, architects, bankers, engineers and lawyers. As one likes to say, they make something of themselves. They seldom if ever get into trouble. Why should they? They have learned in their childhood that order can also mean success. They never forget their musical childhood. They are wide awake and critical at concerts: an excellent, strict audience.

An entire generation of Choir Boys was sent, still by Rector Schnitt, into the diplomatic service. Many a consul or chancellor at an Austrian embassy is a former Vienna Choir Boy. A chancellor is the cashier, takes care of tax stamps, the mail and the contact with Austria. Chancellors are the most important civil servants overseas. As a former Vienna Choir Boy one usually has the addresses of other former Choir Boys who can be of assistance.

On closer scrutiny it would appear only right that Vienna Choir Boys seldom are geniuses, but usually grow into good citizens. It would almost be suspect, if the Institute were the breeding ground for the extraordinary. It is a positive sign for the undisturbed childhood of the Vienna Choir Boys that they grow up to become decent human beings.

Even though there rarely is a large meeting of former Vienna Choir Boys, diverse groups have formed. One is informed about one another, about those who sang before, and about what the active boys do now. It would be quite simple to put together an anniversary convocation to which at least one representative of every generation since 1924 would some. It would be a formidable group and could be the proof for a steady, quiet, and progressive development.

The visible and sensible changes in the sixty odd years are positive, if one neglects World War II, the setbacks and the reconstruction. Where faith in God was the watchword during the founding times, there now are substituted secure contracts for the future. Where in previous times every sort of job had to be accepted, one now is able to select only the best ones. And it is not the greatest financial gain which determines the decisions, but rather the reputation of the Institute which determines where the Choir Boys are to appear next in concert, in a film, on TV, or on a recording. The spirit of the founding times has not been lost but has been augmented by the good feeling one gets from a sense of dignity. One may easily see it from the buildings around the Augarten Palace. In 1947 the Vienna Choir Boys were able to rent a ruin and to rebuild it with their own means. They earned their rental by renovating the place room by room, and by taking care of the sanitary installations. In 1948 they also took over the Josefstöckl next door, and converted a partially bombed out structure into a building filled with life. Then they erected, with their own initiative, four large new buildings with apartments and rooms for personnel, spacious modern recreational facilities, acoustically isolated rehearsal rooms, and an indoor pool. The property on Lake Wörthersee is complete and large enough for decades to come. Whatever they are, whatever they own, whatever secures their future: all this they have earned on their own through singing. At a time when one even concedes in the USA, that soon it will become impossible to maintain an orchestra or an opera house without state subsidy, the Vienna Choir Boys can look to the future with quiet confidence, secure in the knowledge that their independence is assured.

Neither their monopoly position nor the demand for concerts by the Vienna Choir Boys has diminished. It is said that the world in turmoil, that the old values are no longer valid, that new objectives must still be formulated. But even in such a world there are ever growing numbers of people who love music, who want to hear children's voices, just as Pope Pius XIth who presented to a choir of the Vienna Choir Boys a parchment on which he had written four lines by Schiller: "He hears a sound/like sweet flutes/ like the voices of angels/ in Paradise."

*S*inging in a choir means always attempting something worthwile together.

*T*he Choir Boys learn to perform on stage and they learn the ways of the world.

A Viennese operetta: part of the Vienna Choir Boys manifold repertory.

*T*raditionally costumed Viennese in a ballet? The Vienna Choir Boys of course.

*T*he boys are greatly amused by those things which will
later provide the public with much entertainment.

*R*ehearsals also take place in Sekirn, on the Lake Wörthersee, the summer home of the Choir Boys. Here in Jacques Offenbach's "Monsieur et Madame Denis".

*T*he boys are more often to be found in the water than in costume.
They have the Lake Wörthersee (Carinthia) right in front of the door.

THE TRAVELS
1926–1987

1926	July	Innsbruck
	August	Salzburg, Reichenhall, Switzerland
1927	January	Graz
	February	Carinthia
	March	Graz
	April	Germany
	June	Switzerland, Germany, Vorarlberg
	August	Frankfort on the Main
	September	Prague
	October	Germany
	December	Graz
1928	January	Switzerland
	March	Czechoslovakia
	April	Yugoslavia
	May	Znaim, Budapest
	August	Vorarlberg, Switzerland, Germany
	October	Poland, Germany
	December	Yugoslavia, Styria, Carinthia
1929	February	Czechoslovakia
	April–June	Salzburg, Italy, France, Spain, Switzerland
	August	Salzburg
	October	Tyrol, Vorarlberg, Switzerland, Germany
	November	Yugoslavia
		Norway, Sweden, Denmark, Germany
	December	Graz
1930	February	Germany, Denmark, Sweden, Poland
	March	Greece, Bulgaria
	April	Budapest, Frankfort on the Main
	May	Poland
	October	Salzburg, Tyrol, Germany, Switzerland, South Tyrol
	November	Sweden
	December	Graz

1931	January	Styria, Yugoslavia
	February	Germany, Denmark, Sweden, Czechoslovakia
	April	Carinthia, East Tyrol, Italy
	June	Munich, Graz
	July	Germany, Upper Austria, Salzburg, Styria, Switzerland
	September	Poland, Czechoslovakia
	November	Leoben, Czechoslovakia
1932	January	Graz, Greece, Yugoslavia
	February	Denmark, Czechoslovakia
	April	South Tyrol
	May	Czechoslovakia, Munich
	July	Salzburg, Tyrol, Styria, Carinthia
	August	Tyrol, Germany
	September	Switzerland, Upper Silesia, Sweden
	October	Moravia
	October–February 1933	North America (1rst travel)
	December	Czechoslovakia
1933	March	Upper Austria, Salzburg, Tyrol
	May	Hungary
	July–August	Italy, Czechoslovakia
	September–March 1934	North America (2nd travel)
	September–December	Denmark, Sweden, Finland, Estonia, Latvia, Danzing, Poland, Czechoslovakia
1934	January	Upper Austria, Salzburg
	March	Sweden
	April	Poland
	July	Salzburg (Festivals)
	September–February 1935	North America (3rd travel), Canada
	September–December	England, Belgium, Netherlands, Germany, Lithuania, Latvia, Finland, Czechoslovakia
1935	January and April	Switzerland, Spain, France, Saarland
	April–May	Czechoslovakia
	July–August 1936	Australia, New Zealand, Fiji Islands, Samoa, Hawaiian Islands, North America (4th travel)
	September–November	Switzerland, Netherlands, Belgium

1936	January–February	France
	March–October	Argentina, Uruguay, Chile, Brazil
	April–May	Belgium, Netherlands, France
	June–August	Latvia, Lithuania, Poland, Rumania, Yugoslavia
	September–December	Switzerland, Germany, Netherlands, Belgium, France
	September–December	Sweden, Germany, England, France, Denmark, Danzig, Poland
	December–April 1937	North America (5th travel)
	December	Alsace, Slovakia
1937	February	Austria, Switzerland, Venezuela, Curacao, Puerto Rico, San Domingo, Cuba, Mexico
	March	France, Netherlands, Switzerland
	April	Saarland, Alsace
	October–November	Germany
	October–February 1938	North America (6th travel)
1938	February	Germany, Denmark
	March–April	France, Switzerland, Liechtenstein
	July–August	Germany
	September–December	Switzerland, Germany
	October–January 1939	North America (7th travel)
	December–February 1939	Netherlands, Belgium, Germany
1945	Travels in Austria	Lower Austria, Upper Austria, Salzburg, Tyrol
1946	July–August	Switzerland, Austria
	September	Slovakia, Hungary
	December	Germany
1947	January–February	Germany, France, Portugal
	February–April	Sweden, Denmark
	September	Austria
	October–December	Germany, France
	September–November	Netherlands, Belgium
	December–January 1948	Switzerland
1948	April	Italy
	May	Switzerland, Istanbul, Greece
	July	Austria, Italy (South Tyrol)
	August–January 1949	Norway, Sweden, Denmark, Belgium
	September–March 1949	USA (8th travel, 1rst USA-travel after the war), Canada, France (Alsace)

1949	*January–April*	*Germany, Switzerland, Austria*
	May–November	*South America: Brazil, Uruguay, Argentina, Chile, Peru, Ecuador, Venezuela, Colombia, Panama, Mexico; New York*
	September–December	*Denmark, Netherlands, Belgium*
	October–March 1950	*North America (9th travel)*
1950	*March–May*	*Switzerland, France*
	July–September	*Germany, France (Alsace)*
	August	*Austria*
	August–December	*Hamburg, Norway, Sweden, Finland, Denmark, England*
	September–December	*Germany*
1951	*June–September*	*Germany, Denmark*
	August–December	*Norway, Sweden, Finland, Denmark, England*
	November–April	*USA (10th travel)*
1952	*January-June*	*Germany, England, South Africa*
	May–October	*France, Switzerland, Germany*
	July–December	*Germany, Italy*
	September–December	*Norway, Sweden, Finland, Belgium*
	October	*St. Pölten*
	November	*Enns, Freistadt (Upper Austria), Linz*
	December–April 1953	*USA (11th travel)*
1953	*January–April*	*Belgium, England, Denmark, Germany*
	April–May	*England, Ireland*
	July–December	*Austria, Switzerland*
	August	*Austria*
	August	*Netherlands*
	September–December	*Norway, Sweden, Finland, Belgium*
	November–December	*Italy*
	December	*France*
	December–April 1954	*Germany*
1954	*February*	*Switzerland (together with Imperial Music Chapel)*
	February	*Austria*
	February–November	*Australia, New Zealand, Panama, Ceylon*
	May	*Switzerland*
	July	*Austria*
	July–November	*Germany*

July–August	Austria
September	Germany
October–November	England
November–April 1955	Germany
December–April 1955	USA (12th travel), Canada
1955 March–July	England, South Africa
April–May	Switzerland, Germany
July	Austria
July–August	Germany, Austria, Switzerland
July–December	Germany
August–November	Norway, Sweden, Finland, Denmark, Germany, France
September–November	Netherlands, Belgium
December	Germany
December–April 1956	USA (13th travel), Canada
December–February 1956	Japan (1rst East Asia-travel after the war)
1956 February–March	Switzerland, England, Germany
April	Germany
May	Hungary
August	Austria
August–November	Germany
November	France (Paris)
December-April 1957	USA (14th travel), Canada
1957 January–March	France (Alsace), England, Netherlands
March–April	France
March	Belgium, England
June–August	South America
August	Austria
August	Germany
September–December	Germany
October	France (Alsace), Italy, Switzerland
December–April 1958	USA (15th travel), Canada
1958 January–April	Austria, Greece, Belgium, Netherlands, England, Germany
August	Austria
August	Germany
September–December	Germany
November	England
December	Austria
December–March 1959	USA (16th travel), Canada

1959	March–September	France, Japan, Singapore, Hong-Kong, Kuala Lumpur, Australia, New Zealand
	March–August	England, South Africa
	July–August	Austria
	August–November	Germany, Switzerland, Belgium, England, France
	November	Austria
	November–December	France, Spain, Portugal
	December–April 1960	USA (17th travel), Canada
1960	January–April	Germany, England
	April	Austria
	April	Germany
	July	Austria
	August–September	Germany
	September–December	Germany, Switzerland
	October–December	Germany, England
	December	France (Paris)
1961	January–April	USA (18th travel)
	January–March	Austria, France (Alsace), Belgium, England, Germany
	April	Denmark
	April	Austria
	June	Austria
	August	Germany, Switzerland
	August–December	Portugal, Spain, South and Central America
	August–October	Germany
	September–December	Japan, Formosa (Taiwan), India
	October–December	England, Germany
1962	January–March	USA (19th travel)
	July	Llangollen (Wales)
	July	Netherlands
	July–September	Austria
	August	Germany
	September–November	Germany, England
	December	Germany
	December–April 1963	USA (20th travel)
1963	January–March	Austria, Switzerland, France, Luxembourg, England, Belgium, Netherlands
	April–July	Sweden, Denmark, Germany, Austria

	June–July	Austria
	August	Austria
	August–December	Germany
	September–December	Austria, England, Belgium, France, Netherlands, Spain
	November–December	Germany
1964	January–March	USA (21rst travel)
	February	Innsbruck
	March–September	Asia, Australia
	April	Austria
	May	Austria
	July–August	Austria
	August–December	Austria, Switzerland, Netherlands, Belgium, Germany, England, Denmark
	September–December	Germany
	November	Austria
1965	January–March	USA (22nd travel)
	January–April	England, Switzerland, Denmark
	April	Austria
	May	Austria
	May	France (Versailles)
	July–August	Austria
	August–December	Germany
	October	USA (Texas, Dallas)
	October	Austria
	November	Austria
	November	Rome
	December	Germany
1966	January–April	Austria, Belgium, France, England, Switzerland
	January–March	USA (23rd travel)
	July–August	Austria
	August–September	South America
	August	Germany
	September–November	Germany, England
	September–December	Finland, Denmark, Austria, Italy (South Tyrol), Germany
	November	Hungary
1967	January–March	USA (24th travel)
	February–August	Turkey, Lebanon, Iran, Thailand, Philippines, Hong-Kong, Formosa (Taiwan), Japan

April	*Italy (South Tyrol)*
June	*England*
July	*Austria*
August–December	*Germany, England*
August	*Austria*
September–December	*Austria, Yugoslavia, Denmark, Sweden, Germany*
1968 January–March	*USA (25th travel)*
January–March	*Switzerland, Germany, England, France, Spain*
March–April	*Austria*
July	*Austria*
August	*Yugoslavia*
August–December	*South Africa*
September–December	*Germany, England*
1969 January–March	*USA (26th travel), England, Ireland*
January–March	*Austria, Netherlands, Belgium, England, Spain*
March–June	*Asia, Japan*
June	*Austria*
August	*Yugoslavia*
September–December	*Germany, England*
September	*Netherlands*
December–March 1970	*USA (27th travel)*
1970 February	*Germany*
March	*England*
April–July	*Asia, Australia, New Zealand*
May	*Germany*
May	*Hungary*
August	*Germany*
August	*Austria*
August–December	*Austria, Yugoslavia, France, England, Denmark*
September–December	*Austria, Germany*
December–March 1971	*USA (28th travel)*
1971 January–April	*Austria, Benelux, England, Spain*
April	*Austria*
May	*Switzerland*
July–September	*South America*
September–December	*Germany, England*

September–December	*Sweden, Norway, Denmark*
December–March 1972	*USA (29th travel)*
1972 March	*England*
March–June	*Iran, India, Thailand, Korea, Singapore, Philippines, Malaysia*
August	*Germany*
September–December	*Germany, England*
September–December	*Austria, Switzerland, Germany*
December–March 1973	*USA (30th travel)*
1973 January–March	*Austria, England, France, Spain*
July–October	*South Africa, Kenya*
August–September	*Malaysia, Singapore, New Zealand, Australia, Macao, Hong-Kong, Manila, Formosa (Taiwan)*
September–December	*England, Germany*
December–April 1974	*USA (31rst travel)*
1974 February–March	*England, France, Switzerland*
July–September	*South and Central America*
September	*Germany*
October	*Sweden, Norway*
October	*England*
November	*Denmark*
November–December	*Germany*
November–December	*Netherlands, Belgium, Luxembourg*
1975 December 1974 – February	*America (32nd travel)*
March–June	*Asia*
March–June	*Japan*
August	*Yugoslavia*
September	*Germany*
September–October	*Austria*
October	*England*
October–December	*America (33rd travel)*
November–December	*Germany*
1976 January	*Austria*
January–February	*Switzerland*
January–March	*America (34th travel)*
February	*Belgium*
March	*Denmark*
March–April	*Austria*

	September	Germany
	September–October	Germany
	October	Netherlands
	October–November	Sweden
	November	England
	November–December	Germany
	December	Germany
1977	March–April	Belgium
	March–May	Austria
	April–June	South America
	June	Central America
	June	Germany
	September	Germany
	September–October	Germany
	September–December	USA (35th travel)
	October–November	England
	November–December	Germany
	December	Germany
1978	March	Belgium, France
	March–April	Belgium
	March–June	Japan
	March–July	Asia
	April	Norway, Sweden
	May	Finland, Germany
	May–June	Spain, Portugal
	July	Australia
	August–September	Germany
	August–October	Netherlands
	August–October	Germany
	October–November	Sweden
	October–December	USA (36th travel)
	November–December	Germany
	December	Germany
1979	January	Austria
	January–February	Austria
	January–February	Belgium
	February	Caribbees
	February–March	France
	February–March	USA (37th travel)
	March	Switzerland

March		Austria
August–December		Germany
September		Germany
September–October		Switzerland
October		Greece
October		Spain
November–December		England
December		Germany
1980	December 1979 – April	USA (38th travel), Canada
	January	Austria
	January	Switzerland
	February–March	Germany
	March–April	New York (RCMH-Show)
	August–December	Germany, England
	September–December	Asia
1981	January–March	USA (39th travel)
	January–March	Austria, Switzerland, Belgium, France
	July–August	South and Central America
	August–October	Africa
	September–December	Germany, England
	October–November	Sweden, Finland
	November–December	Germany
1982	January–March	Austria, Switzerland, Germany
	January–March	USA (40th Reise), Canada
	September–October	Germany, France
	September–October	Germany
	October–December	USA (41rst travel)
	November	England
	December	Germany
1983	January	Denmark
	January–March	USA (42nd travel), Canada
	March–July	Asia, Japan, Australia
	September–October	Austria, Switzerland
	September–October	Germany
	October–December	USA (43rd travel)

November	*England*
November–December	*Germany*
1984 January–March	*USA (44th travel), Canada*
January–March	*Austria, Switzerland, Belgium, Germany, Denmark, Sweden*
August–December	*Germany, England*
September–December	*Austria, Spain, USA (45th travel)*
1985 January–March	*Austria, Switzerland, France, Belgium, Netherlands*
January–April	*USA (46th travel)*
March	*Israel*
March	*Austria*
July–September	*South and Central America*
August–September	*South Africa*
August–December	*Germany, Great Britain*
September	*Turin/Italy*
October	*Greece*
October–December	*USA (47th travel)*
1986 January–March	*USA (48th travel)*
March–July	*Asia, Japan*
September–December	*Germany, Great Britain*
September–December	*Austria, Italy, USA (49th travel)*
1987 January–March	*USA (50th travel)*
January–March	*Austria, Switzerland, France, Italy, Spain, Yugoslavia, Israel*
August–December	*Taiwan, USA (51rst travel)*
September–December	*Germany, Great Britain*